RALPH

COFFEE, JAZZ, & POETRY

Ralph Alfonso

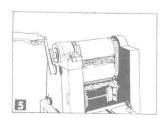

505-1288 Broughton, Vancouver, BC, CANADA, V6G 2B5
TEL: 604-654-2929 • FAX: 604-654-1993

Hello!

I'm Ralph and this is my little poetry monthly. I print it on an old 1940s Gestetner mimeograph machine and try to distribute it to cool stores all over, where you can pick it up for free. This is definitely something different as I pay for everything with earnings from my work as a graphics designer.

Reaction so far has been extremely positive and most stores say that copies disappear within a few days and that people start coming back for further issues.

I guess the philosophy behind what I'm trying to do is that people are bombarded with paper every day which, by and large, is of a temporary nature and thrown away almost as soon as it's picked up. In the midst of all that, I'd like to provide a bit of a change and some creativity you can enjoy and hang on to.

If you like what you see, then I would certainly appreciate your letting people know it's available by placing it in a nice little corner of your shop.
If you do not want copies sent to you, please let me know.

Thanks again for your time and, hopefully, your support.

Take care,

Ralph Alfonso

1993 letter sent to bookstores, record stores, etc.

RALPH (Coffee, Jazz and Poetry) ©1997 Ralph Alfonso.
First printing.

Published by Water Row Press
PO Box 438, Sudbury, MA, 01776

ISBN 0-934953-45-7

All rights reserved. No part of this book may be reproduced, stored in a retrieval system, or transmitted in any form or by any means, electronic, mechanical, photocopying, recording, or otherwise, without the prior written permission of the copyright owner.
Or in simpler terms: You steal my work and I don't eat.
Registered with CANCOPY.

FREE No. 1, November, 1992

RALPH

a journal by & about Ralph

Contains:
- a cool story
- a nice poem
- and MORE!

a new life

She looked out her window at the little squares of light set against the backdrop of a Fall night sky (it always looked darker at this time of the year). The fluorescent checkerboard flickered on the black office towers sprouting skyward out of the horizon before her.

There was something about the early morning that relaxed her, a lunar tranquility that held all motion captive in the quicksand of sleep.

The air seemed purer to breathe, a cool tonic that nestled inside her lungs. It swept through her body with a confidence and a reassurance that all was well in her world; this was a moment to savor.

Her arms folded around her sweater-draped body - shoulder and waist held in place by either hand. Perhaps she'd float away otherwise was her thought.

So much to do. Her brain, fortified by the moment's elixir, was busy organizing and prioritizing.

It was a plan for the new day.

a long kiss in the rain

Wet sidewalks; mirrors for neon lights, empty restaurants, and rain-soaked newspapers kicked out of the way.

We couldn't think of anything to say. She stirred her coffee again. I lit a cigarette. She picked at her cake. I thought, well, what a mistake this was.

At least she smiled when she realized it, too, and held a forkful of crumblysomething at my mouth. I said something funny. I liked to see her laugh.

Just a mild drizzle in the parking lot. I open the car door for her, but before she can get in, I hold her; right there - for a long kiss in the rain.

sleep

Leaves are falling
down
from somewhere
way up there
Tired old trees
shrugging off
their coats
so they can have
a stretch
and
then
just
go
to
sleep.

when

when my heart stopped
beating
It didn't matter
I kept on living

a long walk on the sand

a long walk on the sand
the waves poured in and washed up
alongside our bare feet.
I was so happy to be with her
to stop and look up at the moon
and hold each other for warmth

and i do

I love you so much
I want to hold
and kiss
and let you know
You're my only friend
The only thing I care for
When your heart beats next
to mine
I want to say all of this
and I do

RALPH is published every month and is hand-printed one page at a time on vintage Gestetner duplicating machines (using equally old funny smelling inks) by RALPH ALFONSO.
If you would like to use this antiquated method to enhance your creative process, please call me. Comments, correspondence, requests for more copies to: RALPH, 505-1288 Broughton St., Vancouver, BC, CANADA, V6G 2B5. Oh, did I mention I'm a graphic designer looking for freelance work? Call me for your next cool project (604-654-2929).
THIS IS A LIMITED EDITION PRINTING OF: <u>1000</u>. ©1992 by R.A.

FREE

No. 2, December, 1992

RALPH

a journal by & about Ralph

CONTENTS SUITABLE FOR BONGOS

a cool YULE story & poetry

DANS MON LIVRE

dans mon livre
c'est très simple
roman pas compliqué
dialogue
oui, beacoup
mais de l'amour surtout
tirage limité
et réservé à deux

BEAT FOR THE HOLIDAYS

the fireplace
warm
and you and I
together

maybe there's snow
or maybe not

flames on the candles
melting wax

nighttime - stars are out
and
scratchy records
(real music will never wear out)

drink hot coffee
from a bottomless cup

it's nothing
but it's everything...
if it makes you smile

LEAVES

orange
brown
yellow
and
green
leaves carpet the wet pavement.
that we kick through
we look up; and the empty branches are
set against the evening sky in a jigsaw
pattern and where a leaf has yet to fall,
its black silhouette looks like
a missing puzzle piece.

EVEN INTO MY HEART

They say it's a grey October
as we watch the white surf
rise and splatter against itself
in great convulsions of wind-swept origin.
In the distance, shrouded in the
late afternoon mist, is an island, I don't know
its name, but on its highest surface,
a lighthouse beacon spins an orange swath
in time to some inner heart beat.

As the beam brushed against me,
I had hoped to perhaps feel it;
but it was an intangible element.
Perhaps, in that moment, it had
seeped right through me...

perhaps even into my heart.
(Maybe, in that second,
it had re-set its course)

ONLY TUESDAY IN THE LAND OF AUTUMN

Grey and cold.
It's windy today.
The waves are being swept high into the air; crashing down on the pock-marked sand - sending the gulls spluttering off in all directions.
You can see the odd feather left floating...
spiraling down 'till I brush it out of my way.
I turn around and see that the squawking gulls have settled down into the grooves of my footsteps in the sand
(that's one way of covering up my tracks, I smiled).
Sad little California beach. Where have all the people gone?
It's not the season for people.
The one I want is far away...while I roam through the sand in exile ..
here in my kingdom of nothing.
I call upon my subjects...hey, get your beaks out of the garbage cans...I'm talking to you!
Lift yourselves into the sky. Do something useful for once.
It's Christmas. I could use a little Christmas.
I throw a rock at them; and the misshapen cloud of scurrying scavengers mushrooms up towards the horizon.
Smoking a cigarette at a beach cafe; I could see the empty bodies of the California people moving the lips on their identical heads. Empty of anything useful to anyone; what could they possibly be talking about?
The Mexican beer slid down my throat into an appreciative belly.
My cynicism certainly thrives in cold weather, doesn't it? I liked it better when I didn't know as much to let it betray me
(victim of my own environment).
The last surfers were straggling up the beach; boards in tow.
The sun was about to set. Time to go home.
Something hits my head and bounces onto the table.
I look next to the ashtray.
It's an ugly green and silver Christmas tree ball!
Those stupid gulls. Always showing off.

RALPH is published every month and hand-printed one page at a time on 50s-era Gestetner screen duplicating machines (using equally vintage inks) by RALPH ALFONSO. Layout and typeset on a MAC IIcx. Laserproof originals are then scanned on either a 50s or 60s-era (I have both) Gestefax drum scanner which simultaneously cuts a plastic plate that is placed on the duplicating machine's silkscreen. Ink is hand-squeezed onto the ink-rollers during printing. Yes, 90s software working together with 50s hardware, it is possible. This issue's paper stock is recycled Genesis Milkweed. If you would like to use this antiquated method to enhance your creative process, please call me. Comments, correspondence, requests for more copies to: RALPH, 505-1288 Broughton St., Vancouver, BC, CANADA, V6G 2B5. Oh, did I mention I'm a graphic designer looking for freelance work? Call me for your next cool project (604-654-2929). I'm fast & I'm cheap. THIS IS A LIMITED EDITION PRINTING OF: 1000. ©1992 by R.A.

FREE   No. 3, January, 1993

RALPH

COFFEE, JAZZ, & POETRY

Chet baker

Sunday at Newport

A high hat and a simple snare
A bass line that is almost there
A whisper from an angel's mouth
Is a song that fills the air

We never spoke
But I lit your cigarette
As we sat on the grass
Nodding our heads to the music

We were in heaven
And I was with you

...with fifty Italian strings

full moon
could be June
cool girl
could be soon
when we get to kiss
hold her hand
understand
that this could be love
from above
just like in books
could be novel
with a happy ending
cause
it's got
a happy beginning

Paris in September

Paris in September
these are moments to remember
A lazy walk
through a Paris park
A quiet coffee
in a corner cafe
We must be in love
(you know - a waiter can tell)

I've got the best seat
right here next to your heart
There's the river below
The Eiffel Tower above
and jazz blowin' in
from the club down the street

Some drinks after dark
holding hands while we talk
We'll make this our song
This is where we belong
In Paris
In September

RIFFIN'

Got a note, Blow a note
Wrote a note, Quote a note
Sent a note, Read a note
Saw a note, Drop a note
Change a note, Play a note
Flip a note, Float a note
And on this note...
please add your notes

Chet baker's Cigarette

is hanging from his
Italian girlfriend's mouth.
They're both here in
a little club
sitting at the back table
Chet is drinking something
maybe coffee from a tiny cup.
She laughs
and he smiles
his sweet smile
just like the William Claxton portraits
on the back of his albums.
His skin is tight
his mouth is perfect
The blond American
California cool.
He leans over to whisper something
She laughs some more
drags on the cigarette and
passes it back
and it slides into his mouth.
In that instant
it's like he's out of his body
he sucks in sweet smoke
his blue eyes fixed
in contemplation
It's a second that's a lifetime
that he finds solitude in
because he's inside
with the perfect notes
waiting to be blown
And these happy Italians
and everybody
there will always be distractions

But no one will ever know
what it's like
here inside
and
as long as he can hold his horn
he can keep them all away
with
the pretty music

Now she ruffles up his hair
and tickles the side of his neck

He exhales
a fine grey mist of smoke
and puts out the stub
in the little black ashtray.
He combs his hair back in place
because he's back in the world
and it's time to be distracted

RALPH is published monthly and hand-printed one page at a time on 50s-era Gestetner duplicating machines (using equally vintage inks) by RALPH ALFONSO. Layout and typeset on a MAC IIcx. Laserproof originals are then scanned on either a 50s (tubes!) or 60s-era (integrated circuits) Gestefax drum scanner which simultaneously cuts a plastic plate that is placed on the duplicating machine's silkscreen. Ink is hand-squeezed onto the ink-rollers during printing. Yes, 90s software working together with 50s hardware, it is possible. This issue's paper stock is recycled Genesis Milkweed. Chet Baker photo by William Claxton is from the back of a World Pacific lp by Bud Shank & Chet Baker. This is the quintessential Chet portrait. The bottom right corner typeface is a custom font created by myself with help from my brothers John & Nick Alfonso. It is a tribute to the cool hand-lettering of 50s French & Italian jazz albums and posters.

Comments, correspondence, requests for more copies to: RALPH, 505-1288 Broughton St., Vancouver, BC, CANADA, V6G 2B5. My machines and/or my design skills are all for hire. Drop me a note for a quote! THIS IS A LIMITED EDITION PRINTING OF: 1200. ©1992 by R.A. Distributed by hand or by mail to cool people & places all over. I'll mail you a copy every month if you send me 12 stamps or monetary equivalent.

FREE   No. 4, February, 1993

RALPH

COFFEE, JAZZ, & FEB. 14

love

ALL THE ABOVE

the girl I love
is all the above
and even more
I can't ignore
there's just no limit
certainly
no end
she's one of everything
but most of all...
my friend

20 LITTLE KISSES

1.
A
rainy night
is
another excuse
to
hold you
tight.

2.
A kiss
beneath
your umbrella
will
always keep the rain away

3.
There will always be
lips
to kiss
There will always be
eyes
to look into.

4.
walking through the red
leaves
crunching up the ground
makes you wonder
what a funny sound!

5.
The highway to your heart
it's taken many detours
before I got to the start

6.
The best thing
about
seeing eye to eye
is
being
mouth to mouth

7.
Your touch on my heart
is what makes it start

8.
It wouldn't be winter
without a fireplace
and you

9.
when you hold my heart
please be careful
don't let it drop

10.
Leaves on the trees
shake with the breeze
and flutter down
upon the ground
where
we share a kiss
on a night like this

11.
I can honestly say
that anything that may have
made me sad
has gone away
since being with you

12.
Walking in the park
is always a good excuse
for holding hands

Sitting on a bench
is always a good excuse
for...
a kiss

13.
A lot of things
seem less important
now
that I have found you

14.
No matter
how bad a day it's been
as long as
there's your smile
at the end

15.
Winter in your arms
is
an eternity of warmth

16.
Sometimes
the touch of our lips
is more
than what our mouths
could ever say

17.
Our lips touch
That's the start
Our hands
Our hearts
Each do
Their part

18.
I let you hold on
to my heart,
It's very small
for such a major part.
It never falters
and never stops,
I trust you with it
As you can tell
So always watch it
and treat it well.

19.
Listening to our records
Lost in a better world
when Love
was a kiss
and
a quiet whisper

20.
I know...
Sometimes, I don't make any sense
but
it's the thought that counts

IT HAPPENS

Sometimes..
and I know this happens
I suddenly decide
to call you

And you suddenly decide
to call me

And
we can't get through
to each other

AND SO
IN THIS BEGINNING

In this beginning
For which there is no end
There are only blank pages
to re-invent ourselves
There is no history
No past
No previous misconception
Every day is the future

JUST SO

If I smoked,
I'd light up a cigarette
Just about now
While I waited for
the coffee to cool down

And then you'd sit down
wrapped in your white housecoat
And if you you smoked
You'd put a cigarette to your mouth
And I
would light it

And then I would say something funny
Just so
I could see you smile

AT THE TOP OF THE WORLD

The blue neon signs
shed a pale light on the
snow-covered streets
that you and I are walking through
watching the little mists of
cold air float up every time
we speak

And in this wonderful place
At the top of the world
in these empty streets
we stop under a street lamp
and we hold each other tight
we kiss
But it's so cold -
our lips stick together.

AND THEN

The morning after
our first night
we stare at each other
sheepishly
and then
we smile

RALPH is published monthly and hand-printed one page at a time on 50s-era Gestetner duplicating machines by RALPH ALFONSO. This is my first annual Valentine's Day issue. Copy one of these poems onto a blank card and make someone you love smile, or better yet, give them the whole thing (write your personal note in the blank space above). Comments and correspondence to: RALPH, 505 - 1288 Broughton St., Vancouver, BC, CANADA, V6G 2B5. My machines and/or my design skills are all for hire. Drop me a note for a quote! THIS IS A LIMITED EDITION PRINTING OF: 1200. ©1992 by Ralph Alfonso. Distributed by hand or by mail to cool people and places all over. I'll mail you a copy every month if you send me 12 stamps or monetary equivalent. Back issues are $1.00 each.

FREE No. 5, March, 1993

RALPH

COFFEE, JAZZ, & POETRY

Vince Taylor

ALIAS VINCE TAYLOR

Sometimes French people just bug me. Or maybe it's just the Parisians. This was the second time in two days that the desk clerk at the hotel had corrected me when I tried to say my room number in French.
He did it in a rude condescending way like I was some little kid.
Lucky for him I hold my temper well.
So I started to hang at the bar, wondering how French women manage to hang on to their looks, or at least maintain this illusion, cause when you get right close, there is a very unreal quality to their tautness.
Too much cigarette smoking, probably.
Anyway, I thought I'd made a cool discovery in Stella Artois beer and after a long day of wandering around Paris, I'd unwind with a few at this little hole in the wall place inside the hotel. Sometimes I'd end up talking to people in my own sort of simple French. I had some vague notion about possibly running into a totally beautiful French artiste/existentialist who was blonde and dressed mostly in black that would guide me through the smoky jazz demi-monde of Paris.
Maybe I'd read too many books about this.
Anyway, I was starting to get intrigued by this one character who'd always drop in around midnight; slide into the back corner table and coolly, meticulously, pour back some man-style drinks.
For some reason, I was sitting at the next table one night when he must have caught me looking his way.
"You a musician?" he asked...in English.
"No...sorry...," I stammered.
"You should be," he said. "You got the look."
Up close he looked older, maybe in his forties...but well-preserved. We talked for a little about very trivial stuff. Maybe I made a crack about French people in general.
"Yeah," he said, "But, on the other hand, if the French like you, they stick with you when everyone else forgets."
He let that kind of hang...and then sipped on his drink, his eyes staring straight ahead, almost like I wasn't even there.
I don't know how I hadn't noticed before, but he was wearing skin tight black leather racing gloves, the kind that cut off at the palm of your hand.
A gold I.D. bracelet glinted around a wrist. Why hadn't I asked before?
"Are you a musician?" I asked.
His lips curved into a smile.
"No, I'm not a musician," he said. This time he looked right at me.
He clinked his glass against mine.
"I'm a rocker."

FRANCOISE HARDY'S JACKET

It was her lips.
Or maybe it was her pout.
The picture of her and Brian Jones.
Her long blonde hair. Her white boots.
Her soft thin voice on precious songs of love.

Did she look like Mick Jagger?
Why did they call her the "yeh yeh" girl from France?
She sang in French. She was cool, smart and
fashionable in a very mod sort of way.

I found her records in flea markets and for 99¢ in
the back bins of second-hand stores. She even
sang in English; in a charming fragile kind of way.

I guess it was the black alligator jacket that always
sticks in my mind. Shiny, almost leathery,
it hinted at a worldly maturity that
few of her peers would ever grasp.

Just like Diana Rigg's jumpsuit.
But that's another story.

ROCK SLOW TWIST SURF

Quand le Jukebox est plein
on danse vers le matin
avec Chuck et Bo
Hey, Hey
What'd I say

Le monde c'est ma blonde
Je l'embrasse pour un slow
Yeah, man
That's heaven to me

Cigarettes, belles lunettes
Chaque heure c'est un fête
C'etait partir de l'ambiance
Twist a St. Tropez

When the jukebox is on
we're gonna dance till dawn
with Chuck and Bo
Go Man Go
Hey, Hey
What'd I say

That girl is my world
and when we dance slow
Yeah, man
That's heaven to me

Cool shades, make it louder
We keep a'rockin' every hour
That's the way it's gotta be
Twist at St. Tropez

SALUT LES COPAINS

Johnny, Claude, Dick et Vince
Sylvie, Stone, France et Francoise
Chats Sauvages, Chaussettes Noirs, blousons noir
Antoine rencontre les Problèmes
Lucky Luke, Lucky Blondo
Rocky Volcano, Dany et les Pirates
Long Chris, Adamo, Tintin et Spirou
Quatre garçons dans le vent
et vous
et moi

FRANCOISE SAGAN

Francoise Sagan is a French writer I like a lot mostly because of her economy of language. Her books are really slim and it's funny to see how various publishers try to puff them up with big type, blank pages between chapters, extra long catalogue listings at the back, etc.

She is mostly known as a worldly 18-year-old, who, in the mid-50s, wrote BONJOUR TRISTESSE, a little book of sexual tension that rocked Europe and made a little noise in America. It was quickly transformed into a not very good movie with David Niven. The best part of the picture is when Juliette Greco sings. You also cannot take your eyes off Jean Seberg. This woman is a cinematic icon and it's really only the French who knew that sometimes with Seberg, dialogue wasn't really necessary to convey what had to be said. Directed with the heavy hand of Otto Preminger, BONJOUR TRISTESSE is a good example of everything bad about early 60s American cinema.

Sagan's early work is her best; A CERTAIN SMILE, AIMEZ VOUS BRAHMS, and THOSE WITHOUT SHADOWS. Some are still in print on Penquin. Beware, tho, some of her later prose has been "Harlequinised" by some American publishers. The 50s paperbacks have cool covers.

She was the quintessential young French existentialist and marketed directly to the American bohemian crowd. There was a real craze for "French" novels in the late 50s (mostly girls coming of age stuff - the singular French theme it seems), but Sagan's were innocent little jewels in the midst of it all. I hope you will discover her work as she is a point of reference for me.

Oh...both Francoise Sagan and Francoise Hardy have the same first name. Both wore black. Both were French. Hardy's songs had minimal lyrics and Sagan's books had not a lot of words. They both would have known who Vince Taylor was and may have met him perhaps at a party. Sadly, there are no references to any such encounters in any of their various published biographies. We can only imagine the conversations.

This issue is a tribute to 60s French rock'n'roll and its primary icons; Johnny Hallyday, Vince Taylor, Françoise Hardy. Clad in head to toe black leather, Vince Taylor (a transplanted Briton) was the personification of early rock's primal sexuality to a generation of French, and best known as the writer of "Brand New Cadillac". A 24-track compilation of his work is available in Canada via Polygram records. Buy it. Lots of pictures of Vince in leather and chains. Gene Vincent was a boy scout next to this guy.

RALPH is published monthly and hand-printed one page at a time on 1950s Gestetner duplicating machines by RALPH ALFONSO. Comments and correspondence to: RALPH, 505 - 1288 Broughton St., Vancouver, BC, CANADA, V6G 2B5. My machines and/or my design skills are all for hire. Drop me a note for a quote! **THIS IS A LIMITED EDITION PRINTING OF:** 1000. ©1993 by Ralph Alfonso. Distributed by hand or by mail to cool people and places all over. I'll mail you a copy every month if you send me 12 stamps or monetary equivalent. All back issues are $1.00 each (and going fast!). Your support is welcome and appreciated. Later.

FREE No.6, April, 1993

RALPH

COFFEE, JAZZ, & POETRY

blue april

Astrud Gilberto

23

A SENTIMENTAL TEAR IS NEVER A SURPRISE

A sentimental tear
Is never a surprise
But I never would have thought
to see one from your eyes

A LOVE SUPREME

A sweet thought
of a gentle kiss
The hole in my heart
of a part I will miss
The best love
is always
a lost love
That's the beauty of
a love supreme

WILL THERE EVER BE APRIL

Will there ever be April
It's a month I understand
When rain washes down
I sink into sand

LE BLEU DU MATIN

Si l'heure a du couleur
c'est bleu
et s'il manque du bonheur
il y'a du bleu
et s'il avait un cœur
c'est bleu
et s'il trouve des choses perdues
c'est nous

For every hour
there's a colour
and it's blue
and if there was a heart
it's blue
and if there's something to be found
it's you

CIAO RAGAZZI

Finitto la guerra
Di giornatti di blu
Addio la vita
Cosi breve con tu

WE THINK TOO MUCH

Sometimes
in life
we think too much
about
the simple things
like just
a touch

BLUE APRIL

Sometimes
It seems
Every raindrop is blue
and
My world sheds a tear
When I'm without you

I always thought
I could ride out the storm
But
It's not true
I guess even sunshine
Starts out as blue

Well, I wish
I could find
Something to do
But
You can't do much
When your April is blue

A TICKET TO HEAVEN, BABY

A ticket to heaven, baby
Well, that would be nice
Having a coffee
Up in Paradise

UNWRAPPING THE BANDAGES

And so, here we are
I've travelled by land
You've driven by car

It's funny how
we struggle for words,
choosing each one for
precision and clarity of
meaning
There must be no misunderstanding
No subtext or interpretation

Sometimes it's best to
let the wounds heal
unwrap the bandages
and
let the skin feel
the world again

WHEN ASTRUD GILBERTO SINGS

When Astrud Gilberto sings
The sun cuts through the rain
Everything's quiet
And I feel happy again

WHAT'S NEW IN THE WORLD OF RALPH:
Look for the new CD by Huevos Rancheros on the cool C/Z Records label. Photography and design by yours truly. The music is raw and totally instrumental. On the complete opposite end of the musical spectrum, I just did the same for the new West End Girls, all-girl pop on Johnny Jet Records. Alas, I am still waiting for my first jazz project. Could it be you?

Cover photo by Jerry Schatzberg
from the album "Beach Samba" on Verve.

RALPH is published monthly and hand-printed one page at a time on 1950s Gestetner duplicating machines by RALPH ALFONSO. Comments and correspondence to: RALPH, 505 - 1288 Broughton St., Vancouver, BC, CANADA, V6G 2B5. My machines and/or my design skills are all for hire. Business calls only to: 604-654-2929 or FAX: 604-654-1993 (both are work numbers). **THIS IS A LIMITED EDITION PRINTING OF:** 1200. ©1993 by Ralph Alfonso. Distributed by hand or by mail to cool people and places all over. I'll mail you a copy every month if you send me 12 stamps or monetary equivalent (IRCs outside North America). All back issues are $1.00 each (and going fast!). Let me know of any cool stores I should be mailing RALPH to. Thanks and.............later!

FREE No. 7, May, 1993

RALPH

COFFEE, JAZZ, & POETRY

MYSTERIES OF LIFE

It's My Nervous System

It's my nervous system
I know it's making my muscles twitch

These days I can only relax
when I'm driving my car
I don't know why

It's usually dark
when I go through the city
except for the buildings
They always look green
for some reason

I don't know what I'm thinking
about usually
My head just opens up
I guess the best thing is
I like listening to the radio
and drumming along on
the steering wheel
Sometimes maybe I try singing
But I make sure the windows are closed
if I'm going to do that

Life's Mysteries (Part 1)

The waitress laughs
It's been a long time since someone
asked about the neon sign
that doesn't work

Or why the menus are on
pink paper

But -
If we don't order soon
We might miss the Breakfast Special

A Large Coffee

So I sat down
Maybe there were two other people in there
I asked for a large coffee
I always put in two sugar substitutes
plus two milks - it tastes just like
there was real sugar in it

I guess one of the great mysteries
to me, anyway
(I don't know, sometimes everything's
a mystery to me)
has always been
how the donut shop
has become such an oasis of comfort
But, more importantly,
why do people end up buying
more muffins than they do
donuts?

If We Could

The television is flickering
The bowls of fruit are empty
We didn't drink everything we
brought out, so now
The bottles are all over

The remote control has fallen
to the floor
The video boxes are stacked
in a corner

There's probably a lot more
of the same, and we'd straighten
it all out if we could
but...
we fell asleep on the couch

The Quality Of Happiness

Sitting
Here
Watching the green waves
crash upon the sand
which is wet and caked like moist
earth
I'm distracted by some children
boisterous in their commotions

I'm thinking of my future
The quality of happiness
The extent of the emptiness
The sacrifice for the pursuit
of an unspecified goal

And then I think about
your friendship
And sharing in your warmth
And I know that all is for the better
now that I've found you

I Can Never Find A Place To Eat

I can never find a place to eat
when I'm driving around
It's crazy
And it makes my girlfriend nuts
And if we do spot something
I can't find parking
So
I'm back in the doghouse
But it's not so bad
At least I can smoke here

Language Falls Apart

I see you everyday
But I don't know what to say
Every time I start
My language falls apart
This is something I don't understand

Words I Put In Your Mouth

Little
crumpled marionette
I met you in that ancient
shopkeeper's window
I liked the way
your head hung over
your chest
weighed down by gravity.
I'm sure you were once
a European nobleman of
grand lineage
Maybe princesses
laughed at your stories
or listened in awe
to tales of great adventure
as you scaled the Pyramids.
Your ruffled shirt is grey with dust
that flies about
as I lift you up
The strings straighten out
my hands pull them tight
There is pride in your construction
A majesty of manner and grace
A certain bearing
as you walk the stage again
The words I put into your mouth
will never be what's in your heart
and that is my only regret.

Static Keeping Rhythm

Tadpoles hopping across the wet road
Rain dumped out of some giant bucket
Windshield wipers helpless
against the onslaught
On this dark northern highway
With radio static keeping rhythm
Over the hills and around the bends

It seems like hours
Maybe it's been a lifetime
But soon the water will stop
And probably, so will I
I don't know how to drive
any other way

YOU CAN ALWAYS ASK RALPH:
Some people have actually asked if I write all this stuff myself.
The answer is, quite unexpectedly, yes.
I had always thought it was rather evident, but for the record;
unless otherwise noted, everything is written and/or drawn by yours truly.

SOME SPECIAL THANK YOU'S:
To the following for your nice reviews;
Judith Beeman, Manny Goncalves, Hal Kelly, & of course,
FIZ for reprinting a poem & spelling my name completely all wrong.

RALPH is published monthly and hand-printed one page at a time on 1950s Gestetner duplicating machines by RALPH ALFONSO. Comments and correspondence to: RALPH, 505 - 1288 Broughton St., Vancouver, BC, CANADA, V6G 2B5. My e.mail address is: ralph6982@aol.com. My machines and/or my design skills are all for hire. Business calls only to: 604-654-2929 or FAX: 604-654-1993 (both are work numbers). **THIS IS A LIMITED EDITION PRINTING OF:** 1500. ©1993 by Ralph Alfonso. Distributed by hand or by mail to cool people and places all over. I'll mail you a copy every month if you send me 12 Canadian stamps or monetary equivalent ($5 in the USA & 12 x IRCs outside North America). All back issues are $1 ea. Read more, it's good for you.

FREE No. 8, June, 1993

RALPH

COFFEE, JAZZ, & POETRY

ANGELS FALL FROM HEAVEN

THE PACIFIC OCEAN

It was a fine white mist
that hovered around her
as the waves kept crashing down
one after the other in a steady
rhythmic crescendo almost
orchestral in its nature

She was sitting on a mound of
black rock planted in sand,
facing the Pacific Ocean,
conducting her symphony and
reveling in the scope of
its complexity and grandeur

Wind and fowl and vegetation
swirled, swooped and swayed
to her grand majesty.
Almost a primal umbilical...
or better yet, like she was perched
atop the very aorta of
all around her

She had never really believed in a
greater power, but now found it
hard to refute that there was a
higher order of which everything is
an integral part

ANGELS FALL FROM HEAVEN

Angels fall from
Heaven and I
don't know why

All of them
they fill the evening sky
and in that crowd
are
you and I

THESE ENDLESS HOURS

Baby
There's bright colours
And we're walking
Holding flowers
And all through these endless hours
I love you

LONG DISTANCE TO GOD

I wish it could be that simple
You pick up the phone and call him.
Leave a message with his receptionist
and maybe he'd get back to you
before the end of the week, depending
I guess, on the nature of the call.

Of course, he didn't necessarily have
to phone back; sometimes it was
usually pretty obvious that he'd
helped you out. As long as you said
thank you, everything would be
great. Not that he's one to take back
anything, but you'd probably have
to try just a little bit harder next time.

VISITOR

In the Cathedral
of
Missed Opportunity
I am a visitor
of
great regularity

LOST IN THE RAIN

I'm always wandering
lost in the rain
I can never find an umbrella
or a raincoat
I always look like I've fallen
overboard
at the end of the day
with my moppy wet hair streaming
down my face
But today,
as I stepped out from under
an archway
I found you...
and the rain
while it still poured
meant more.
Because in the world of my thoughts
I was being cleansed
for a new beginning
with you...

YOUR WONDERFUL LOOKS

Your wonderful looks
they used to fill
so many wonderful books
But now
it's too late to find
what God gave by chance
ruined by human hands

MOMENT OF REVELATION

In this moment of revelation
My eyes are open wide
And I see that you've
been here all along
It was normal to be blind
I didn't know it was wrong

MESSAGES FROM HEAVEN

Messages from Heaven
Well, here they come again
Sometimes when I'm lonely
They are my only friend

I don't know who it is
That sends them to me
But I'm grateful
For the chance to see
How little things
Like love and kindness
Will bring me to
the goodness of your heart
And everything else will
always follow
It's better to not question
All these messages from Heaven
Well, here they come again

MY MEMORY OF BRIAN

My memory of Brian
is always of
a conscience that
some had wished
they had

YOU ARE EVERYWHERE

You are everywhere
I see your smile
I see your hair

You're all around me
All above

It must be magic
when it's love

Front cover photo of yours truly by Tom Robe.
Shot on location at the portals of Hell,
The Rex Hotel, Queen St., Toronto, 1979.
That beautiful white silk shirt was later dyed black.

RALPH is published monthly and hand-printed one page at a time on 1950s Gestetner duplicating machines by RALPH ALFONSO. Comments and correspondence to: RALPH, 505 - 1288 Broughton St., Vancouver, BC, CANADA, V6G 2B5. My e.mail address is: ralph6982@aol.com. My machines and/or my design skills are all for hire. Business calls only to: 604-654-2929 or FAX: 604-654-1993 (both are work numbers). **THIS IS A LIMITED EDITION PRINTING OF:** 1300. ©1993 by Ralph Alfonso. Distributed by hand or by mail to cool people and places all over. I'll mail you a copy every month if you send me 12 Canadian stamps or monetary equivalent ($5 in the USA & 12 x IRCs outside North America). All back issues are $1 ea. Read more, it's good for you.

FREE   No. 9, 1993

RALPH

COFFEE, JAZZ, & POETRY

relatively, beat

SUNSHINE FOR FLOWERS

So many bright lights
in this city without night
we spoke words
we found in
little translation books
But one silent walk
holding hands
said so much more
So many people
it didn't matter
when we kissed
They all went away

When your eyes
looked over
your little pink cup
I had to smile

There's always jazz on the jukebox
when you drink coffee in Tokyo
maybe Verve, or it's Blue Note
maybe Arlen or Porter
doesn't matter the order
It's sunshine for flowers
In Winter, in Love.

IT'S A WONDERFUL WORLD
(if you know someone in it)

I guess
I'm a paid up member
of the lonely club
A connoisseur of
the cigarette stub

And
in life's parade
if I'm a clown
at least you're smiling
when I'm around

Yes
it's a wonderful world
if you know someone in it
it's a wonderful world
if you know your place

A HAPPY PLACE

Cigarettes are unhealthy
and
coffee's a potent brew
But I'd gladly have them both
if it meant being here
with you

Your smiling face
A happy place
Our rendezvous...
And darling
Wherever you are
I think of you

VENUS IN (VIOLETS FOR YOUR) FURS

Excuse me, but
You hold that cigarette well
In fact, I think I'm in love
I feel my little heart swell

Can I have a seat?
Share a coffee or two
I can't believe I'd say this
But I think I love you

We talked for hours
Til they shut down the place
The way that you smile
You send my heart into space

How could we have lived
And not met before?
I've made it to heaven
And you opened the door

I'M JUST HAPPY BEING HAPPY HERE WITH YOU

Well, let the world keep on spinning
Let the winners keep on winning
As for me, I'll keep on swinging
I'm just happy being happy here with you

HOW BEAUTIFUL IS NIGHT

Aah...
Comme c'est belle la nuit
C'est l'amour qu'elle conduit
et quand je pense a toi
Alors, c'est comme ça
je t'aime
et
voilà

Aah...
How beautiful is night
Stars guide young lovers in flight
And
darling, whenever I think of you
it's love and
it's right

*in homage to Robert Farnon

YOU DON'T HAVE TO BE AN EINSTEIN TO DIG JAZZ:
More lyrics to bop melodies that don't exist (yet), in loving tribute to scratchy old records that I like. Not as easy as it appears. The advent of greed has meant most musicians would rather write both music & lyrics for more publishing royalties, so consequently nobody is writing cool new songs for all these new coiffed vocal stylists, so therefore I'd rather spend my money on the real thing like Julie London, Ella, Frank, etc. (altho I did dig Vic Godard's 1982 "Songs For Sale" lp). Check out RALPH #3 & #6 for more of the same.

RALPH RECOMMENDS:
Two brilliant new CDs featuring the orchestral arrangements of the extremely obscure (to us anyway) Robert Farnon. One is **FRANK SINATRA SINGS GREAT SONGS FROM GREAT BRITAIN** (Reprise), worth it just for "If I Had You" (the subtlety of instrumentation is mind-boggling); and **GEORGE SHEARING WITH THE ROBERT FARNON ORCHESTRA:** *HOW BEAUTIFUL IS NIGHT* (Telarc). Hey, if Frank digs this guy, you should, too.

COVER ILLUSTRATION:
Drawn exclusively for **RALPH** by the ultra-cool Scott Saavedra, creator of such comic book classics as *IT'S SCIENCE, JAVA TOWN,* and *DR. RADIUM.* Send him stamps for his newsletter/catalog of cool stuff (tell him I sent you so I can keep being his pal). Scott's coolness is doubly elevated because of his knowledge of the lost art of applying zip-a-tone (sorry, artistes, I don't think they make it anymore). Scott Saavedra, 19411 San Marcos Rd., Saratoga, Ca., USA, 95070

RALPH is published monthly and hand-printed one page at a time on 1950s Gestetner duplicating machines by RALPH ALFONSO. Comments and correspondence to: RALPH, 505 - 1288 Broughton St., Vancouver, BC, CANADA, V6G 2B5. My e.mail address is: ralpha6982@aol.com. My design skills are for hire. Business calls only to: 604-654-2929 or FAX: 604-654-1993 (both are work numbers). **THIS IS A LIMITED EDITION PRINTING OF:** 1300. ©1993 by Ralph Alfonso. Distributed by hand or by mail to cool people and places all over. I'll mail you a copy every month if you send me 12 Canadian stamps or monetary equivalent ($5 in the USA & 12 x IRCs outside North America). All back issues are $1 ea. Read more, it's good for you.

FREE   No. 10, 1993

RALPH

coffee, jazz, & poetry

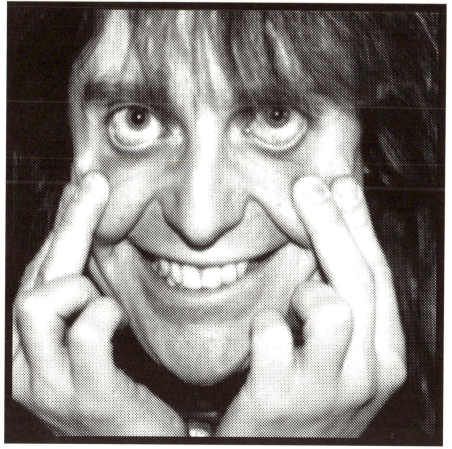

AUGUST TRAVELS

it would be great to
wake up in a place where
we didn't know where we were

It would be great to
wake up in a place
where we didn't know where
we were
or how we got there
and I wouldn't really care
I see your wonderful face
and I want to hold
and kiss you for a long time
Our room would be white
the bed full of exotic pillows
A warm morning sun
making the sky blue
and large windows open
to the view
of a pretty city
where no one seemed to live
except us
Maybe we'd laugh a little bit
and wonder
what was going on,
but maybe just for a second.
It's not that important
And I'm sure there would be music
Some quiet violins
and a gentle baroque piano
coming from a little garden
we can see
of red and orange
yellow and blue
white and green flowers
Did I say our room had
beautiful bouquets in white wicker baskets
Well,
it does.
I have no idea who made this world
But I'm grateful
they made you.

crawling around in the fountain

It's way past midnight
I have no idea what I had been drinking
but, man, was my brain on a
rocket to the moon
which, incidentally, is
practically the only light I've got
here right now
knee-deep and flailing around
in this fountain in the middle of Rome
looking for the pennies I threw
in here
years ago, with this girl
it turns out
I hardly knew
Man, I lost some really good wishes
that never had a chance
to come true
So I figure, hell, I'm here
If I can get those coins back
I can try again
next time I've got something in mind
for the future
But
now I'm completely dripping wet
and some woman is yelling at me
in crazy Italian from some window
up the street
And I'm thinking, oh no
not now
when I slip on the guck
and swing my hands out in front of me
so I don't hit bottom
and I grab a bunch of coins and
run splashing down
the little cobblestone streets
with two cops giving chase
But it doesn't matter
I found my little Canadian penny
And now I'm back at the start

the beauty of
stuff i don't understand

Looking up at the mountains in Hope
I'm thinking, man, they're big
And I'm just hanging here
like some mope
overcome by the beauty
of stuff I don't understand
But I do know one thing
I should've bought one of those
panoramic instant cameras at the drug store
instead of bringing this contraption
I barely know how to use
Well, whatever
I go walk down by the river and take
close up photos of the nice flowers
I can't help but laugh
these people are probably going
Hey, what kind of tourist is this?
Wait till they see this poem, eh?
I wonder if any beatniks ever made it up here
in the 50s?
Can you imagine?
"Hey pops, how's the fishin'?"
"So, this is a cow, eh? So, what do I do, like,
bring my coffee cup over and squirt some
milk in, or what?"
"Hey, you boys aren't making fun of me, are you?"
"No way, dad, they just don't teach us this stuff
in college, like this Square Dance on Saturday,
for example, like, we've been trying to figure
this out, like,
just exactly how do Squares dance?"
Well, it might have been like that.
I don't know. I dig it here.
The physicality of this town is not important
The spirituality is where it's at, but,
just don't stand in one place too long
going "cool" -
it looks kinda goofy.

love@this_destination

we met late
one night
on each other's
screens
we thought
we were worlds apart
but after you
had corrected most of
my obvious misconceptions
of how things work
according to you
and I conceded defeat
you laughed, well,
actually, you typed
"ha, ha, ha, :)"
and I said, well, I'm gonna
pour myself a coffee, cause
we do that a lot in Vancouver
and you said, "No way!
I'm in Vancouver, too!"
and next thing you know
I'm knocking on your door
with a big pot of coffee
and a bag of cookies
extra chocolate chip,
because
well,
we'd circled round the globe
to find...
you live upstairs

AUGUST TRAVELS:
Driving to a different city is always an adventure. Last month I went to about 6 different cities in a week, ending up with a really nice weekend in Seattle, where I bought stacks of books and all kinds of cool magazines. I was also one of maybe 60 people in the audience to see Penelope Houston in a Seattle club. Man, she's great! Older punk historians will remember her fronting The Avengers but this new music is very roots. Too bad her CD is really hard to find.

RALPH RECOMMENDS:
Hey, the new CD by Steve Allen, *PLAYS JAZZ TONIGHT* (Concord Jazz) is a really great workout of old jazz tunes. It's totally instrumental so you can sing, read, or bang along on some cardboard box and really get the neighbors going! Remember, there would be no Kerouac box set without Steve Allen.

WHEN IN VANCOUVER:
Visit **THE UNICORN** pub/restaurant (weekends are wild). I designed the menus & art-directed the new interiors. I can do the same for you. Remember, this publication is made possible only by money I make as a freelance designer/photographer. Choosing between food and a tube of rare brown ink is a tough decision (as you'll note from this issue, the ink won). And don't forget **THE ARTEMESIA GALLERY** at 7th & Main (I actually got an invite in the mail and they were really nice when I dropped by, and poured me a coffee, too!).

COVER PHOTO:
Yours truly photographed at the Grand Hotel in Oslo, Norway, 1986, shortly after a delightful breakfast of fresh herring on toast. For the next 3 years, I would live in a little bunk on a tour bus with various rock groups who graciously provided me with the opportunity to explore this wonderful planet so I could share my harvest of nice moments here and there with you each month.

RALPH SAYS:
Wonderful things are all around you.
Open your eyes. Trust your heart.

RALPH is published monthly. Written & hand-printed one page at a time on 1950s Gestetner duplicating machines by RALPH ALFONSO. Correspondence to: RALPH, Box 505 - 1288 Broughton St., Vancouver, BC, CANADA, V6G 2B5. My e.mail address is: ralpha6982@aol.com. My design skills are for hire. Business calls only to: 604-654-2929 or FAX: 604-654-1993 (both are work numbers). THIS IS A LIMITED EDITION PRINTING OF: 1300. ©1993 by Ralph Alfonso. Distributed by hand or by mail to cool people and places all over. I'll mail you a copy every month if you send me 12 Canadian stamps or monetary equivalent ($5 in the USA & 12 x IRCs outside North America). All back issues are $1 ea. Read more, it's good for you.

FREE   No. 11, Oct. 1993

RALPH

coffee, jazz, & poetry

SO,
I OPENED
THE DOOR
AND
SOME BONES
FELL OUT
AND
HIT ME
ON
THE
HEAD

WHAT'S ONE MORE SIN WHEN YOU'RE ALREADY IN HELL

I thought if I slapped her, everything would be all right; that she'd come out of her stupor and I'd be able to hold her in my arms and forget that all of this happened, but it was too late now.

When I got up the next morning, she was still lying on the floor, crumpled up like some piece of paper. I lifted up the blanket I'd put over her and felt the purple bruise where her mouth used to be. I knelt down and brushed my lips against hers.

Sometimes when we used to kiss, I would softly pull away the hair from her face and run my fingers through it.

So it was no surprise when she left; when I let her go. From the apartment balcony I could see her walk through the park. She stopped to sit on a swing and looked up.

When I sat on that little wooden swing later that day, I reached down to pick up one of the Fall leaves. I held it for a long time until I let go and the wind lifted it away.

THE GIRL WITH MY LAST NAME SHE USED TO BE MY WIFE

I guess enough has been written about the dirt in L.A. About the illusion of L.A. Just about enough has been told already. But not enough about my ex-wife. The one that left me. Right there, on the beach in L.A. Well, maybe I guess it was a fight. I'm not sure. The back of my head still hurts a little bit. That's where the radio hit me after she threw it ... I've got the stupid thing right here. It still works, except sometimes the stereo cuts out. Oh well.

It was supposed to be a vacation, but I ended up doing work stuff and she'd come along to some of these business lunches and mope and make the odd crack.

So I got her the car and gave her the map and said, "So listen, go shopping or something, and I'll see you later".

Maybe, in her mind, that was the last straw. Who knows? It's been five years of this, I thought, I was glad to see her go.

So that was last year. A couple of months after we split, I thought, maybe I'll call her up and say hello. So, some guy answers the phone! I hung up. I couldn't believe it!

I spoke to her for the first time maybe a week ago. Things seem to be going ok with her and "him". I forget his name, but people like him bug me. So he's living with my ex-wife, I don't care. Really!

It's almost Christmas. Do you think I should send her a card?

LETTERS SENT

So many letters sent
So many words of love
Set to flame with each
new match
that's struck

AWKWARD CONVERSATION

It's hard to look at lips
You know you can't touch
A mouth you once tasted
Is now just a smile
You must return
Out of nervousness

The awkward conversations
That try to bridge the past
Sound shallow
On reflection

But words are precious
In their scarcity
And each phrase laboured
For complexity of meaning

MY TABLEAUX OF HAPPINESS

The logic of desire
is a formula for deceit

My tableaux of happiness
is a canvas by the blind

WAITING IN THE LOBBY AT THE DETOX CENTRE

This is where my baby lives
She used to live with me
But now she's dead,
Or pretty close
And this,
Well,
This is her ghost
I try to talk to her
But my words go right through
And sometimes
I wish I was smarter
So I'd know what to do

THE SENSE OF TOUCH

And these
These are my fingers
That are on your lips
It's the sense of touch.
It's one of five
That the two of us
Seem to be missing
Some of.

WHEN

when my heart stopped
beating
It didn't matter
I kept on living

WHEN I REACHED INTO THE CLOSET FOR MY JACKET, I DIDN'T EXPECT TO FIND A SKELETON IN IT!

I thought I would exorcise some demons this month, since it is October. All of this material was written in California in 1986 (a really miserable year, all in all), with the exception of "Waiting In The Lobby" which is from this year. I'll get back on track next month, but in the meantime, have a bad coffee, crank up that first Nico album... and don't open any doors until November!

RALPH RECOMMENDS:

Over the summer I contributed to two very interesting projects that are worthy of your attention. The first is an incredible book that mixes various media (color photocopying, rubber stamps, color slide inserts, etc) into a really cool narrative. LOVE LETTERS TO MADMEN is by Elissa Joy and available for $7.95 (add $1.50 for postage) from Pas De Chance, Box 6704, Station A, Toronto, Ontario, Canada, M5W 1X5. If you like the Griffin & Sabine books, this is their dark side. Designer/Publisher Ian Phillips has created the coolest artist's book in a long time. Yours truly contributed 4 pages of Gestetner printing (definitely my best work as a printer). In keeping with our October motif, the book features lots of eerie pumpkin heads & very cool spiderweb onionskin sheets!

If you were wondering where to submit your poetry, stories & art, may I recommend PRODUCTS OF CONCEPTION, c/o Bart Campbell, 1550 Kitchener St., Vancouver, BC, Canada, V5L 2V9. The first issue is just out and is yours for $3; it features poetry by yours truly who also designed & printed it on Gestetner. Special thanks here also to Bart for his invaluable help and for actually experiencing the sheer non-glamour of helping me print.

COVER PHOTO:

That old photo of me on issue #8 got such nice comments that here is another from the same session at the Rex Hotel, Queen Street, Toronto,1979. Photography by my good friend Tom Robe (416-979-1057) who is an exceptional photographer with very reasonable rates. He has recently been re-discovered by the new Toronto music scene and they are better for it. I have probably known Tom since I was a weird comic fan putting out crazy fanzines with this very same machine. Nothing's changed really, has it?   Cover photo © 1979 by Tom Robe.

RALPH SAYS:

If you're in trouble, ask for help.

RALPH is published monthly. Written & hand-printed one page at a time on 1950s Gestetner duplicating machines by RALPH ALFONSO. Correspondence to: RALPH, Box 505 - 1288 Broughton St., Vancouver, BC, CANADA, V6G 2B5. My e.mail address is: ralpha6982@aol.com. My design skills are for hire. Business calls only to: 604-654-2929 or FAX: 604-654-1993 (both are work numbers). THIS IS A LIMITED EDITION PRINTING OF: 1500. ©1993 by Ralph Alfonso. Distributed by hand or by mail to cool people and places all over. I'll mail you a copy every month if you send me 12 Canadian stamps or monetary equivalent ($5 in the USA & 12 x IRCs outside North America). All back issues are $1 ea. Read more, it's good for you.

FREE No.12, Nov. 1993

RALPH

coffee, jazz, & poetry

FALL IS MY FAVOURITE

fall leaves

Fall leaves come tumbling down
Spinning round
Till they're kicked by you
Picked up by you
And put in a pocket
by you

and there in the doorway

As the rain pours down
As the windshield wipers flail
at the oversized hail
that batters down
on the wet grey car
that snakes through
the pools of water streets
on a mission to your heart

And there in the doorway
Holding onto my umbrella
is
your smile

it's a vancouver day

it's a Vancouver day
although what does that really mean?
maybe a grey sky
empty beaches now
kind of soggy sand
bunch of birds flitting around
dog loping by
choppy water hitting the shore
there are *some* footsteps
because
while there may be no one else
there is still
you and I

kicking at the leaves

kicking at the leaves
in the park
orange, yellow, red, brown, rust
watching them swirl up

and then
a little yellow one
sort of flutters
down
onto your shoulder

some quiet place

Running in
out of the rain
into some quiet place...

The coffee's steaming
so we have to wait for it to
cool down

But that doesn't mean we
can't start digging into the
cheesecake already

And
looking out the window
watching the water run wild
makes me glad
I'm inside
with you

in the safety of your heart

In the comfort of your arms
is where I want to be

In the warmth of your world
is where I want to sleep

And in the safety of your heart
is where my soul to keep

city shutting down

A little seagull wanders by...
Sitting on the beach
You and I

The sun sinking in the Fall sky
The wind brushing through the sand
And nothing else
Just you and I

The silence of the city shutting down
Autumn leaves
Both red and brown

And maybe it's my heart
That lets out a little sigh
He's so happy
It's just you and I

coffee on an autumn day

There's something
about an autumn day
that makes you want to have a coffee

And sit on a park bench
mittens wrapped around a hot cup
sipping through a plastic lid

And watch the world go by
Leaves fall down
Squirrels hunch up and frown

And then
to see you walk towards me
scarves windswept high
Your suede jacket pulled snug...
clutching tight to your
steaming little cup of...
tea

the ocean at night

Sitting in the front seats
of a car
Facing the ocean at night

Watching the waves
crash against the shore

Listening to the sounds of the surf
and the wind
gently rocking the car
every now and again

I don't know about you
But for me
it's the perfect excuse
for
a kiss

there you were

And so the rain poured down
And as it hit the ground
I heard

That in the middle
of all this sound
there you were

No longer lost
but found

autumn night

whispers in the darkness
eyes open wide
but we can't see

just hold out your hand
guide my fingers
to your mouth
so that my lips can follow

ONE YEAR LATER

Exactly one year ago, I published the first issue of this modest publication. It brought me back full circle, after a rather long detour into the music industry as a professional slimeball (well, maybe I'm being too harsh on myself), to the world of fanzines & self-publishing - where I originally came from to begin with.

I spent most of the 70s hunched over this Gestetner machine cranking out an almost endless stream of poetry, comics, rock & everything in-between zines. When Punk broke in 1976, I became one of many rock/comics fans managing a punk band (in my case, THE DIODES). From there, I somehow infiltrated the mainstream Canadian music industry and, simply by being awake, managed to leave a very odd legacy behind me as I hop-scotched from one cool job to another.

Anyway, one day I just quit everything & ended up on a rock in Tofino, BC, staring at the ocean & thinking it's time to get back on track, haul all these dusty old machines out of storage & figure out how they all worked again.

It has been a positive experience all in all. I have no idea where it will lead to; that's part of the adventure. I just try to word my thoughts succinctly & hope each issue can stand on its own as a little body of work & evocation of a particular mood & feeling.

This publication is free because I really don't want to deal with the hassle of money. Luckily, I have a job with understanding employers & I can scrape together enough money each month to pay for ink, paper & postage. Your subscription in stamps or cash is always appreciated & will guarantee a copy to your door.

So that's my story in a very small nutshell. I'm looking forward to another year of publication and whatever else may lie ahead. Trust your heart.

FALL IS MY FAVOURITE

Sometimes I really miss Fall in Montreal; walking through NDG Park; having a hot chocolate up in the Chalet when there's no one around; wasting time at Cheap Thrills looking for old records...but there's also Fall in West End Vancouver & kicking through leaves on a foggy day; taking the little blue boat to Granville Island...

FRONT COVER

A Girl. A Hat. A Cigarette. Photographer Wayne A. Hoecherl & I worked together recently & when I saw this portfolio shot of model Lisa Stark, I just knew I wanted it for a cover. Wayne has a great eye for European flavour & is very reasonable. Call him at 604-222-1978.

RALPH is published monthly. Written & hand-printed one page at a time on 1950s Gestetner duplicating machines by RALPH ALFONSO. Correspondence to: RALPH, Box 505 - 1288 Broughton St., Vancouver, BC, CANADA, V6G 2B5. My e.mail address is: ralpha6982@aol.com. My design skills are for hire. Business calls only to: 604-654-2929 or FAX: 604-654-1993 (both are work numbers). **THIS IS A LIMITED EDITION PRINTING OF: 2000** (yeow, my arm hurts). ©1993 by Ralph Alfonso. Distributed by hand or by mail to cool people and places all over. I'll mail you a copy every month if you send me 12 Canadian stamps or monetary equivalent ($5 in the USA & 12 x IRCs outside North America). All back issues are $1 ea.

FREE — No. 13, Dec. 1993

RALPH
coffee, jazz, & poetry

NEW YEAR'S WEEK

Sincerely and yours truly

You crazy German woman
I have no idea what you're trying to say
until we find a common language
that is foreign to both of us
and in infant French
I say,
Have you ever been kissed by an Italian
It's quite wonderful
I know,
I'm one.
You laugh.
In this new land
will wonders never cease.
Somewhere inside
your blonde cascade of hair
we kiss.
It's crazy,
I know.
I mean,
we only just met.

Spinning (I think)

Hey,
we're giggling like schoolkids
over some private joke
that gets funnier the more we drink
this wonderful cheery wine
from a country unpronounceable
to most everyone here
high above the city
in a restaurant revolving
way too fast
(I think)
and now I'm getting you confused
with everyone else I've ever
gotten drunk here with.
Are you Bill or Betty
Are you both
Have a heart
Don't let me start
extolling the virtues of
your leg
that's resting on my knee;
Let's not get kicked out
before we finish the bottle.

CHRISTMAS STOCKINGS

Hey!
I know you
I bought you stockings last week
didn't I?
Right here,
down the street
at this delightful
lingerie shop
filled to the brim
with flimsy bits of fabric
sold at exorbitant prices
to drunks like me
for people like you

New Year's Eve

(Queen & Bathurst, Toronto, 1977)

I'd like to say
how crazy you are
but that's kind
of hard
what with your
tongue down my mouth
and all
right here
in the middle of traffic
waiting for a bus
actually, any bus
that'll take us
somewhere away from
all these drivers
waving and giving me
the thumbs-up sign
"Yeah, uh, thanks!"
She's really cool,
I know,
that's why I'm here

GO, GOING, GONE (baby)

Doesn't matter what highway
and it
doesn't matter what the sign says
as long as
it's not here
Just keep throwing
everything out the window
so we can go faster
(Baby)
Laughing through the trees
and mountains and truck stops and
biscuits and gravy and flags and kids
waving out back windows
till we reach the ocean
but before we do,
through all these seasons
and constant beauty of this
wonderful land
knowing you're beside me
makes me glad
I love you.

NEW YEAR'S WEEK

Well, Happy New Year! Christmas and New Year's Week always blends into a blur for me. Sometimes the sediments of the season are just as noteworthy as the sentiments. For several magical days, the laws of gravity no longer apply to decorum. Be naughty. Be nice. That's my advice.

RALPH RECOMMENDS

Cool discs for the holidays.
For that quiet night, may I recommend a comfy couch for cuddling, a potent beverage of your choice (a pleasant Gewurztraminer wine or maybe a big bottle of Bailey's on the rocks) and the following cool CDs:

HAVE YOURSELF A JAZZY LITTLE CHRISTMAS, *Various Artists* (Verve): Originally issued in 1989 & still the coolest. You can't beat Verve, my friends. God bless Norman Granz!

THE SINATRA CHRISTMAS ALBUM (Capitol): Frank also did Xmas lps for Reprise & Columbia (& there's the odd bootleg of radio broadcasts). Whatever you buy, keep the volume at ambient level to maintain the mood.

If you have guests:

HIPSTER'S HOLIDAY, *Various Artists* (Rhino): Weird stuff by Eartha Kitt, Miles Davis, Lena Horne, etc. Sure to get the party going.

CHRIS STAMEY & FRIENDS, *Christmas Time* (ESD): Chris collects Alex Chilton, Big Star, Syd Straw, the DB's & more for a very cool jangly pop effort. Chris Stamey is an understated musical treasure. Discover him now. Hey Chris, give me a call, I'll design your next cover for FREE.

For nuzzling in bed the morning after:

GLENN GOULD, *Conducts Wagner's Siegfried Idyll* (Sony Classical): Gould's conducting debut is also his final recording. Very subtle. Very beautiful.

FRONT COVER

Holidays mean fun. Yours truly sleeping it off the morning after. Digital self-portrait using the ever-accommodating LaCie Silverscanner II. That cool font on was created by moi to celebrate my new facial hair and is appropriately called Goatee.

RALPH is published monthly. Written & hand-printed one page at a time on 1950s Gestetner duplicating machines by RALPH ALFONSO. Correspondence to: RALPH, Box 505 - 1288 Broughton St., Vancouver, BC, CANADA, V6G 2B5. My e.mail address is: ralpha6982@aol.com. My design skills are for hire. Business calls only to: 604-654-2929 or FAX: 604-654-1993 (both are work numbers). **THIS IS A LIMITED EDITION PRINTING OF: 2000** (it's a long night). ©1993 by Ralph Alfonso. Distributed by hand or by mail to cool people and places all over. I'll mail you a copy every month if you send me 12 Canadian stamps or monetary equivalent ($5 in the USA & 12 x IRCs outside North America). All back issues are only $1.00 each.

FREE   No.14, Jan. 1994

RALPH
coffee, jazz, & poetry

JANUARY'S A GOOD TIME FOR JAZZ

january's a good time for jazz

It may feel a little cold
tonight
but I don't mind
In these winter moments
I find
January's a good time for jazz

You poor baby your
lips are all blue
They just need a good kiss
and it's true
January's a good time for jazz

but first it starts with a kiss

Breakfast on the balcony
Somewhere
On a beach in France
Dinner in the kitchen
Anywhere
Maybe up to chance
Doesn't matter
where it is
I always know
how it ends...
But first,
it starts with a kiss.

that's the moment that I fall in love

From the moment that
The sun will rise
And lift the sleep
Out from your eyes

That's the moment
That I fall in love
And that's the moment
I thank God above
For you

From the minute that
You say hello
And stretch your arms
You're all aglow

That's the minute
That I fall in love
And that's the minute
I thank God above
For you

all that I know

In life's adventure
I always find
It's best to go forward
with an open mind

In matters of love
This is all that I know
Just follow your heart
And try to go slow

All over the world
Young lovers must kiss
And God made the stars so
We could see this

c'est où le bonheur

C'est qui le roi
dans ce monde
de rêves perdus
C'est qui l'auteur
de ma vie...
J'aime pas l'histoire

C'est où le bonheur
les sourires
et les
fleurs

Who's the king of
this world
Who's the author
of my life...
I don't like the story

Where are the flowers
And those happy hours
I should be sharing
with you

the day we met the week we spent

Who knows
Where or why or when

The day we met
The night we kissed
The week we spent

We're guilty of it all
and more,
it's true
That's the story of
a love brand new

I'm not afraid
to write the book
A million words
for how you look

The day we met
The night we kissed
The week we spent

We're guilty of it all
and more,
it's true
That's the story of
a love brand new

RALPH RECOMMENDS

FRANK SINATRA, *Duets* (Capitol):
Frank returns to the Capitol studios with many of the same musicians (and charts) he first re-defined swing with in the 50s. The set smokes; Frank is in fine form but as for his singing partners, well, if you had ever thought that none of these people could really sing...you are still correct. With the exception of Tony Bennett (a real professional who seems to be the only one actually having a good time here), the rest of these people are about as exciting as a chunk of romano cheese (even Frank Jr. can top these duds). Once the hype dies down...it would be great for Capitol to release a version of this CD with just Mr. Sinatra's complete vocals.

CHARLIE WATTS , *Warm And Tender* (Continuum):
The Charlie Watts Quintet with The Metropolitan Orchestra and vocals by Bernard Fowler. Here are 16 amazing tracks meticulously assembled from the heart by a real fan of romantic 50s jazz. Everything is first-class, including the incredible packaging (hey, Charlie was an art director previous to joining the Stones). It may be a little hard to find, but worth every penny. In its quiet understated way, this is, by far, the best solo Stones album.

FRONT COVER
Drawn exclusively for this issue by the incredible Tom Bagley, currently based in Calgary, Alberta (right in the middle of Canada, eh?). Tom notes David Stone Martin as an influence and I only wish I had music to go with the words inside such a cool cover. If you are a big shot art director, it would serve you well to send Tom a big bag of money and help get his work out there. Cool calls only to: 403-284-3504.
Tell him I sent you so I can still be his pal when he's famous.

NEXT MONTH:
Ring The Bells!
Tribute to THE KINKS!

RALPH is published monthly. Written & hand-printed one page at a time on 1950s Gestetner duplicating machines by RALPH ALFONSO. Correspondence to: RALPH, Box 505 - 1288 Broughton St., Vancouver, BC, CANADA, V6G 2B5. My e.mail address is: ralpha6982@aol.com. My design skills are for hire. Business calls only to: 604-654-2929 or FAX: 604-654-1993 (both are work numbers). THIS IS A LIMITED EDITION PRINTING OF: 2200 (my arm is numb). ©1993 by Ralph Alfonso. Distributed by hand or by mail to cool people and places all over. I'll mail you a copy every month if you send me 12 Canadian stamps or monetary equivalent ($5 in the USA & 12 x IRCs outside North America). All back issues are only $1.00 each.

FREE   No. 15, Feb. 1994

RALPH

coffee, jazz, & poetry

KINKS
KONTROVERSY
KONTINUED...

BEAT
IMPRESSIONS
OF
THE KINKS

I'M ON AN ISLAND

You came out of the crowd
and
I saw you there
Under your umbrella
in Soho Square

Oxford Street is always
noise and light
But here
there's only whispers
in
the quiet
of night

IT'S TOO LATE

I can see the ocean
through the floorboards
at Brighton Pier
I can see
the both of us unhappy
sitting here
Baby, I wish I had the world to give
But
now you know I don't

This sad honeymoon
The little bride and groom
After the cake's all gone away

It's cold
Do you feel it
Baby, please don't cry
wipe your tears on
your mother's wedding gown
Try not to be sad
There's still beauty
in the sun going down

YOU CAN'T WIN

Let's not argue
in someone else's kitchen
Why talk
when we don't listen
I wish I had a cigarette
But
Our kid is on my case
I'd give him a slap
But
I can't
He's got your face

WHAT'S IN STORE FOR ME

My happy Queen
How wonderful you are
I was born in your Empire
In the last wistful days
of its fading star

For the ideals of England
You took away my name
Whatever heritage I claim
was a burden of shame
I was taught in your language
And groomed to be the same

How noble the mission
How proper, how grand
How disciplined the child
no one wants as a man

Set adrift, these new lands
We were left in the sands
Sinking down with no hands
to pull us out

So here I am
No longer of use
to yesterday's plans
And as for tomorrow
When my parents speak
I don't understand

For my blind allegiance
I take all the blame
I would love you my Queen
But you're not the same

RING THE BELLS

My England
Only lives in those charming books
Upstairs at Foyles
Where no one looks

My England
Is clear waters in St. Austell Bay
And sunsets over Cornwall
At the end of day

My England
Is only memories
that have faded beige
When Victoria ruled over Empire
In a Golden Age

I AM FREE

Sometimes, Brian Jones will stop and light up a cigarette down at World's End, the wind coming in and circling round before it spins off, tousling up his blond hair but it always falls back in place, our Brian, he washes it twice a day.

Today, he's wearing the striped sweater he nicked from the Pretty Things house on Chester St., and a red flowing scarf; he'll be wearing it all on the cover of the next Stones EP, the photo shoot is starting in two hours over at Gered Mankowitz' place.

You could always talk to Brian and it was always surprising that he could speak, because you were so used to just seeing him as a photograph, but he was quite clever, being from Cheltenham and all, altho when he got drunk down at The Speakeasy, it was just best to leave him alone, otherwise you'd be involved in some complicated rigamarol that wasn't worth knowing about.

Now, he's with a pretty blond girl dressed all in black and they're walking down to the embankment to look at the boats, whisper, talk, and maybe kiss.

It's always pleasant Mondays on the Chelsea Road.

WHEN I SEE THAT GIRL OF MINE

I thought it was quite nice
Some lovely plates of pasta
Down the wine bar
Wonderful Hampstead rain, isn't it?
I was surprised to discover
You were a hostess in a Soho bar
A French Maid outfit was your costume
Drunk businessmen bought you drinks
That you quickly poured into
convenient plants - that was the
trick wasn't it? How long before
the £50 for the bottle of weak
champagne - that was the game.
Spend, Spend, Spend
You little squinty-eyed rabbits
What an interesting profession, I said
More wine?

WHERE HAVE ALL THE GOOD TIMES GONE?

Lurching about on Putney Bridge
Late at night
Shoving wet chips in my mouth
Glistening with vinegar
(woof - don't let me look down the water)
Blind instinct leading me
Up to Parson's Green
Where the flatmate's mad
I kissed some girl he fancied
A beautiful dancer I will never see again
Except for a letter
From South America (I think)
She's probably out of show-biz now
Married her agent
Feeding the twins somewhere in Hounslow
Sweet dollops of baby pap stuffed
into their mouths
Maybe my letters somewhere in a drawer
Nostalgic recollections
But I can't think about the future now
After all, these days, I'm a pleasant clerk
In an army surplus store
Down the road from Capital Radio
But not tonight
I'm still a long-haired beat group boy
Dancing all night with a Mary Quant girl
And I must say...
Of all the shades kissed for this test
I love purple on my lips the best

MILK COW BLUES

Railway station
Destination
woo wooo Bakerloo
A pleasant collection
Of mostly empty pints
I can't stand to
Wait alone
So here we are
Work is done
Time for home
A bit of fun
Then up and at it once again
Bright and early
Morning train
I think about my blessed life
All the kids
A suffering wife
I fought the battle
But the battle won
Now I just get on with it
Thy will be done

GOTTA GET THE FIRST PLANE HOME

I kissed you at the Fair
You taste like the cotton candy
We ate there
The little ferris wheel
That spins around
And all the laughter
For the clown
We argued every night
Since then
I should have paid attention when
You were in love
While I pretend

THE WORLD KEEPS GOING ROUND

I get lost on Sundays at Camden
I don't know if
I'm in or out or where or when
So many stalls full of life's ambitions
Now all for sale at
Just a quid for ten
And these days,
With me around,
London's just another lonely town

The silly postcards I like to send
If they reach you
I don't know how or why or when
I always smile and maybe just pretend
That things are fine
And I am on the mend

TIL THE END OF THE DAY

It's funny now
walking down Carnaby Street
Sunday morning
Nobody here, I guess
I always stop to look
in the window at Shelly's
I love those boots
Especially the grey suede

I breathe this Spring air
and it fills my lungs
I touch the ground
And I wait for the spirit
Of what you were
To lift my purple heart

Sitting here on the curb
Pushing my collar up
against the wind...

I'm not alone

BEAT IMPRESSIONS OF THE KINKS

In a recent interview with GOLDMINE, Ray Davies said *Kontroversy* was his favourite Kinks album. Coincidentally, it is also mine. The early American Kinks lps not only introduced me to the singularly frustrating and also rewarding songwriting of Ray Davies, but also to the work of Ed Thrasher, the exceptional Reprise Records art director. Not only did I want to conjure up little emotional snapshots like Mr. Davies but I also envied the photography & design of Mr. Thrasher (excellent name, also!).

It is in humble homage to Ray Davies, that, using only the song titles as a starting point, I have written a series of poems, a kind of cycle, inspired by The Kinks *Kontroversy* album. Kind of like beat impressions of a beat group (a play on the various definitions of "beat", depending on what country and in what context). I got the original inspiration from Oscar Peterson's *Jazz Portrait of Frank Sinatra* (Verve). It always comes back to Frank, doesn't it? Funny how Reprise was Frank's label, too (the Canadian Kinks albums, by the way, were issued on the obscure Allied Records label).

When I was in England in 1979, having a pint at a railway station with my friends, The Barracudas, we spotted Ray Davies sitting by himself at a table, invisibly observing the world going round. We debated going over but, by the time we'd worked up the courage...he was gone.

The majority of the situations in these vignettes are from actual experiences. The night I was drunk on Putney Bridge, I was coming back from a big Mod Ball (1979) during the height of the first Mod revival. I returned to Putney years later to see The Pretty Things in concert, but that's a whole other story.

FOR THE MEMORY OF:
Stan Demonsky; A Good Heart In A Wretched Life.
Hope you're making a lot of noise up there.
God bless this earth on which we trod. God bless us all, we are the Mods.

FRONT COVER
Cover illustration by the author in a kind of EVERGREEN REVIEW homage.

NEXT MONTH:
Angels, Arts & Letters

RALPH is published monthly. Written & hand-printed one page at a time on 1950s Gestetner duplicating machines by RALPH ALFONSO. Correspondence to: RALPH, Box 505 - 1288 Broughton St., Vancouver, BC, CANADA, V6G 2B5. My e.mail address is: ralpha6982@aol.com. My design skills are for hire. Business calls only to: 604-654-2929 or FAX: 604-654-1993 (both are work numbers). **THIS IS A LIMITED EDITION PRINTING OF:** 3000 (go for the gusto!). ©1994 by Ralph Alfonso. Distributed by hand or by mail to cool people and places all over. I'll mail you a copy every month if you send me 12 Canadian stamps or monetary equivalent ($5 in the USA & 12 x IRCs outside North America). All back issues are only $1.00 each.

FREE   No.16, 1994

RALPH

coffee, jazz, & poetry

ANGELS, ARTS & LETTERS

I BLESS THIS DAY YOU GAVE ME LIFE

I don't know why you came to see me
But I suppose that it's this season
and that's a good enough reason after all
For an angel to pay a call
and pull back up
someone like me
and mend the wings I broke
during my fall
I thought that they'd forgotten
all about me
It's been so long
I didn't remember who I was
It was hard to re-claim my innocence
Because without it
I wouldn't recognize you
For what you really are
I'm glad you let me hear the choir sing
high above this earth
watching our bodies sleep.
I bless this day you gave me life
so I could fly and spread your light.

BREATHING

I've never had my eyes open
under water before
But it's too late to think about that now
I've already jumped in
and I'm drowning
I can't breathe
because my lungs are full
of the nectar of heaven
I never expected to
sink so fast
I can see everything
so clearly
But I can't do anything
about it
Because I really don't want to
I've never prayed to God before
and I'm sure it's too late
for any answer
I've never hit the bottom before
and I didn't realize
you can still breathe
when you get here

THE BLOWS OF GOD'S CHISEL MAKE US PERFECT

It's a question of Faith
in something smaller
A beating heart
that can't go any farther
It's a question of love
for something greater
you can't fit inside
this life's theatre
It's a question of why
For everything given
Something
is taken
And I wish
that one day
You'll let me
have it all
Without question

I'VE GONE BLIND AND I GOTTA DRIVE ALL NIGHT

Jesus
Show me how to work this light
Cause I've gone blind
And I gotta drive all night

Jesus
Why was I never told
My brakes don't work
On this bumpy road

Jesus
Please take my steering wheel
Cause I'm too scared
And that's how I feel

There are no stops
On my way to Hell
And there's no sign
So I can't tell

I CLEAN THE BOOKS THAT NOBODY WANTS

I clean the books that
nobody wants
Here in the Library
Downtown
on the second floor
I tape the pages
And I fix the covers
And sometimes I'll slip
a little note inside
in the middle
"Thank you for keeping this
book alive by opening it."
Years from now
Maybe
It'll make someone smile

the frailty of language

You found my old pictures
I'm flattered, I guess
You fell in love with
My old clothes
The little smile on my face
I'm glad I meant so much
to your life
For you to follow me here
where I'm just another
old man that's calling you "dear"
I'm glad you brought these old things
They've been out of print for years
Yes, I know, that's what they all say
That my eyes are still the same
Yes, I know about the rest of me
Well, there's only gravity to blame
But, on the other hand
my words have fared better
They're still young and still strong
I'm glad they're on paper
Because that is where they belong

THE GOATEE CLUB

I don't know how I got into this one
Sitting around, drinking beer
with a bunch of weird guys
from The Goatee Club
I thought my life was bad
But not until I met these characters
They're like
A walking sponge of misery
And everybody's kind of checking
each other out
Gotta be careful what you say
It could end up as somebody else's poem

MY SUCCESS AT FAILURE

Is actually a well-thought out
pre-meditated plan
and not
a series of coincidental occurrences
While you celebrate my latest triumph
I will quietly slip through the back door
and
run down the stairs
and grab a cab
and
just keep going

SOME NOTES ON THIS ISSUE'S POEMS:

• "God's Chisel" is a C.S. Lewis quote in reference to that perennial question, "If God is so powerful, why is there pain, etc."

• "I Clean The Books" is a warm hello to Andrea at The San Francisco Public Library. This poem is complete fiction about a job I wish I had.

• "Frailty" was not specifically written about, but, in hindsight, it makes sense to dedicate it to Leonard Cohen. In high school in Montreal, I saw his National Film Board of Canada documentary over & over and I thought anybody who wrote poetry listening to AM rock radio was pretty darn cool. If you're from Montreal, you know what I'm trying to say.

• "Success" well, winner or loser, it's always a good idea to have a plan.

ANGELS, ARTS & LETTERS

I've always distrusted people who flaunt their faith. I hardly ever talk about mine, but lately, it has pervaded my writing in a unique way. You can be agnostic & deal with things all by yourself or you can have faith & get a second opinion. If whatever you do gets you closer to the goodness in your heart, then you're probably better for it. But who am I to tell you how to live your life? I'm still figuring out my toaster.

RALPH RECOMMENDS

Imagine my surprise to get a package from John Giorno, this guy is like an authentic Beat & knew all those guys, etc. His Giorno Poetry Systems is a multi-media concern, releasing all sorts of records, books & more. **GREAT QUEENS WHO LOVED POETRY, by Lita Hornick & Poet Friends**, arrived with no accompanying note. Lita Hornick is a wealthy American collector/patron of the arts who's nurtured poets, painters & others since 1959, & actually has pretty good taste, judging by the color plates of some of the paintings in her collection. The book's title is in reference to her great love for the gay men in her life ("I have never met a dull one"). The bulk of the book is poetic collaborations with the likes of Allen Ginsberg, Peter Orlovsky, Giorno & others. The best part, I thought, was the slim section devoted to her personal credos on collecting, life & stuff. There is no price listed. Write to: Giorno Poetry Systems, 222 Bowery, NY, NY, USA, 10012. Say you saw it here, maybe they'll send me more stuff.

BEN VAUGHN, *MONO USA* (BAR/NONE); In Pop's parade, Ben Vaughn will be perennially sweeping up behind it. When it comes to greasy, oily real American pop culture music, you owe it to yourself to find any of his great CDs on the Restless Records label. This collection of cover songs brings a 60s truck-stop jukebox straight to your house. Worth it for Ersel Hickey's "Goin' Down That Road" alone.

THE HELLO CD OF THE MONTH CLUB: Send them $45 & they mail you a new CD EP every month for a year; by very cool people (Frank Black, Andy Partridge, R.E.M. types, etc). Series curator is John Flansburgh (They Might Be Giants). To order call 1-800-HELLO-41. You can try to scam a free sampler CD by calling Jill Richmond, 201-795-9424, at Bar/None Records in Hoboken (birthplace of Frank). Tell her you saw it here (it can't hurt, plus she has a nice voice).

WE MAGAZINE, CD ISSUE #14: ($8 from We Press, Box 1503, Santa Cruz, CA, 95061, USA). Spoken word collections can be a trying experience, but this one (sent to me with no explanation by Chris Funkhouser, a guy in New York State) is actually pretty decent with 36 tracks of spoken word, jazz, improv & related. The best poet is Andy Clausen; what a great deep boozy voice this guy has.

CHET BAKER, *MY FUNNY VALENTINE* (Pacific Jazz); Original 50s recordings. Great idea for a compilation. Buy it.

RALPH SELLS OUT:

On Dec. 28, 1993, I was a guest on Tom Harrison's CFOX-FM radio show, where I talked (& talked) about my life (yawn), the Canadian music industry (triple yawn), punk rock (1977), and (gasp) even read a poem ("Crawling Around In The Fountain") with a bit of improvised accompaniment. I was very surprised to discover I not only sound quite lucid, but may actually know what I'm talking about (shock!). I will gladly make a copy of this for you (with a cute cover insert) if you just send me $3 to cover the cost of tape & postage (cheap or what?).

FRONT COVER:

The beautiful Xenia Holiday, former lead guitarist for The B-Girls (one 45 on Bomp Records). I took this photo at a rehearsal possibly in 1978. Xenia later appeared on the debut lp by New York's Certain General in the early 80s. This has always been one of my most favorite photographs. Where is she now?

THANK YOU:

For the nice reviews - VOX (Calgary), HOUR (Montreal), BARK (Winnipeg), CELTIC PAMPLEMOUSE, THE EYETALIAN, EXCLAIM (all Toronto), ALTERNATIVE PRESS, FIZ (both USA). If you write about my endeavours, please send a copy ; my telepathic powers aren't what they used to be.

NEXT MONTH:

Gosh, I don't know. It'll be cool. Tribute to Coxsone Dodd coming very soon.

RALPH is published monthly. Written & hand-printed one page at a time on 1950s Gestetner duplicating machines by RALPH ALFONSO. Correspondence to: RALPH, Box 505 - 1288 Broughton St., Vancouver, BC, CANADA, V6G 2B5. My e.mail address is: ralpha6982@aol.com. My design skills are for hire. Business calls only to: 604-654-2929 or FAX: 604-654-1993 (both are work numbers). **THIS IS A LIMITED EDITION PRINTING OF:** 2000 (squeek squeek). ©1994 by Ralph Alfonso. Distributed by hand or by mail to cool people and places all over. I'll mail you a copy every month if you send me 12 Canadian stamps or monetary equivalent ($5 in the USA & 12 x IRCs outside North America). All back issues are only $1.00 each.

THIS ROMANCE

There may be rain
There could be wind
There's always bad weather when
We try to begin
This romance

IT CAN'T GET ANY BETTER

Baby, you know it can't get any louder
When I'm on stage with my Rickenbacker
And baby, you know it can't get any better
When I see you dancing in my baggy sweater

*for Steve Marriot;
(yeah I know he played a Gretsch)

A TOUT CASSER

ci ça fait mal
il faut laisser
les choses que j'aime
c'est a tout casser

and if that hurts
it's best to just let go
the things I love
i've had to throw away

(*pour Johnny Halliday, happy 51st!)

MY DIME

Why should I be paying the price
For what someone else did
Well, we're lovin' on my dime, baby, now
I don't want to smack you like
a pay phone, honey,
but I don't think I'm getting through
Why am I calling long distance
when I'm standing here
next to you

OPPORTUNITIES IN MISERY

You're an opportunity in misery
I can't pass by
You're a wild romance
That will leave me high and dry

You're an empty promise
A telephone that rings
With no reply

You're an opportunity in misery
I can't pass by

You're the laugh in a dream
I wake up to
You're everything I own
Thrown up to the sky

You're an opportunity in misery
I can't pass by

SUNDAYS AT THE STEM

Sundays at The Stem
restaurant
I would have breakfast
with a girl who hated me
I'd stare out the window
at Queen Street in Toronto
and pray I could lift out of my body
and be somewhere else
But I couldn't
Sundays at The Stem
I felt like the little harried waitress
squinting through her thick glasses
running around trying to find
grapefruit for all the wonderful
monied people in black who refused
to eat greasy food at a diner
One day I got fed up and
yelled at one of them to
shut up
and poured ketchup all over their food
took the mineral water away
and made them drink all my coffee
people applauded
my girlfriend left me
and I never had to pay for coffee again

THIS DOMINION

Drunk up on the hill in St. John's, Newfoundland, watching the waves hit the rocks below, stopping on the highway because there's a giant moose in the road, crawling in and out of every bar on that street, you know the one I mean, baby, this proud dominion, on the boat to Charlottetown, that Sunday flea market, you knew I wasn't from there, was I, and all these Nova Scotia backroads, quiet hamlets God has blessed with Celtic fervour, these cobblestone streets of Amherst, falling asleep on this ferry from St. John, New Brunswick, to God knows where, Quebec City, we kissed in the middle of snow and fortresses, and fireworks in Montreal, Sunday dinners in Elora, Fergus flea market, looking for old records in Hamilton, and Toronto... I miss you baby, but you broke my heart. And so Sudbury, Thunder Bay, Kenora (nice fish), Winnipeg, we walked along the sand no one knows about, I'm sorry you tried to show me your world when I was still trying to figure out mine. But, we all have a place in this great dominion, to live and let its beauty heal all wounds.

THIS KISS IS LIKE

This kiss
is like
a photograph in
the rain
a moment we won't
see again

THIS STRANGE EFFECT

Our eyes meet
But that's as close as we'll ever get
You can't tamper with things
When God made us this way
We're man and woman
But with us
Things don't work that way
But that's my problem
I guess
I want more than our friendship
And I could probably have it all
If I wasn't a man
But it's not my hands that will reach into your
Well of loneliness
I can only make you smile
Someone else will make you laugh

PERFORMANCE

You probably didn't see me
I was sitting in the back.
Everything you did on stage
Made absolutely no sense to me.
Why someone as beautiful as you
Could be involved with such
Caterwauling, I'll never know
You must be a lonely breed,
The Performance Artist.
I felt ill at ease
Knowing I was the only one there
Without a body odour
I was hoping no one would notice.
Maybe it's just envy
From all of us
Filling our endless notebooks,
Maintaining an English language
Hardly anyone reads,
Thanks to your de-construction
Of what's good, what's bad.
But more importantly...
You look pretty pale,
You must not be eating well.

OPPORTUNITIES IN MISERY

I'm happy to say it's been my incredible good fortune to have taken advantage of just about every opportunity in misery that has come my way. There's no lack of material with such a treasure trove of turmoil to dig through. After a while, you can only smile and wonder what could possibly happen next?

CANADA IS A GREAT COUNTRY

For my international readers, you're just going to have to trust me on this one. For my Canadian friends, don't take it for granted, especially if you haven't travelled. Get in a car, hop on a bus, even if you make it to the next town for a day, there's always an adventure or at least a cute waiter or waitress.

MEET RALPH IN PERSON. TOUCH HIS GESTETNER.

On Sat, May 28, from 12 to 5pm, I will be at the SPRING '94 SMALL PRESS BOOK FAIR, at The Western Front Lodge, 303 East 8th Ave. (near Main & Broadway), Vancouver. I will have my Gestetner machine all set up and printing the next issue LIVE! IN PERSON! All my new friends from The Goatee Nation (just kidding, my poetic pals) will be there & it will be an exciting introduction to the world of small presses and self publishing. I visited their last one and that's how I came up with the inspiration for this little oeuvre. I'll probably be stuck behind my table all day, so if you could bring a coffee that would be just amazing! I will be more than glad to talk (believe me, I talk a lot) about the arcanaries of mimeograph printing (Ditto or Rex Rotary - which smells worse?), computer graphics (which is cuter - Quark or PageMaker?), Francoise Hardy (if you look like her, I'll marry you. You can hurt me later), jazz (goatees - chin only or beyond?), poetry (the new traditionalism - deal with it) and of course coffee (call me a truck driver, but $2.50 for something that's mostly steamed milk is not coffee). Oh, and for my new fetish pals (thanks to this issue), call me 60s, but fishnets and baggy sweaters, you can't get closer to heaven than that. Now, if all this won't start a conversation, I don't know what will! See you there! Don't be shocked by my appearance, I now have very long hair and a goatee (I've been described as "biblical" looking).

RALPH ON THE ROAD: SAN FRANCISCO '94

Hey, it's time for my yearly road trip and I will be in San Francisco during the first week of June, being a tourist and looking for old books and records (what else?). If you'd like to get together, just fax, call, write or e.mail me and if you're not a weirdo we can have a coffee, eh? No cults, please, I'm Italian.

SOMETIMES I SLEEP

I've been really busy these past two months designing CD covers (Veda Hille, Paul Dean, Bif Naked, Blackston Gang, Marc LaFrance, Annette Ducharme, Explorers), books (the Music West 94 Conference Program), concert posters (Shonen Knife, Wool), menus (The Unicorn), digital art (*MediaWest* magazine), plus my day job, too. At one point, my hands went completely numb from working at a computer night & day (scary, man!). I'm not afraid of hard work since that is what keeps this endeavour going.

RALPH RECOMMENDS

VEDA HILLE, *Path Of A Body* (Festival Distribution): If Jane Siberry and The Rheostatics were on a record together, they would sound like this. Features cool guitarist Stephen Nikleva (Sarah McLachlan, Mae Moore, Lava Hay, etc) and others. A very good indication of where one faction of current Canadian music is going. CD is $20 and cass is $15. Price includes postage & handling. Order from Veda herself at: Ball Of Flames Productions, 3216 W. 13th ave, Vancouver, BC, Canada, V6K 2V3. Tell her I sent you and you might get a personal note back.

IN HELL'S BELLY is a zine devoted to body modification (piercing, tattoos, branding, and related). How surprised was I when they asked to interview me for their #3 issue! The resulting piece got the technical end of what I do all wrong, but the actual interview is pretty cool plus there's a neato picture of me in my best I'm an intense guy look. Send $2 to: 5809 Main St., Vancouver, BC, V5W 2T1. Younger readers still living at home are warned that there is some stuff in here your parents might wonder about.

COVER ILLUSTRATION

By the extremely cool Tommy Kalichak. The fluid craftsmanship of his male & female forms are what attracted me to his work (surprisingly enough in HELL'S BELLY above) and I am proud to introduce him to you. Everybody's an artist these days, but this guy can actually draw! It's a small world when I discovered Tommy's been an assistant to cult comic artist Ken Steacy (whom I've known since my teens and, ahem, whose art I also helped introduce years ago via my old comic zines & this Gestetrner). Tommy's got various projects on the go, including some upcoming shows of his surreal paintings. If you are a savvy Art/Fashion Director, you will call him now, 604-685-1255.

RALPH is published monthly. Written & silk screened one page at a time on 1950s Gestetner duplicating machines by RALPH ALFONSO. Correspondence to: RALPH, Box 505 - 1288 Broughton St., Vancouver, BC, CANADA, V6G 2B5. My e.mail address is: ralpha6982@aol.com. My design skills are for hire. Business calls only to: 604-654-2929 or FAX: 604-654-1993 (both are work numbers). THIS IS A LIMITED EDITION PRINTING OF: 2500 (10 hours to print!). ©1994 by Ralph Alfonso. Distributed by hand or by mail to cool people and places all over. I'll mail you a copy every month if you send me 12 Canadian stamps or monetary equivalent ($5 in the USA & 12 x IRCs outside North America). All back issues are only $1.00 each.

FREE   No. 18, JUNE, 1994

RALPH

COFFEE, JAZZ, & POETRY
DU CAFÉ, JAZZ ET POÉSIE

dans mon livre

dans mon livre
c'est très simple
roman pas compliqué
dialogue
oui, beaucoup
mais de l'amour surtout
tirage limité
et réservé à deux

in my book
it's pretty simple
not too complicated
dialogue
there's plenty of
but, most of all
there's lots of love
it's a limited edition
set aside for two

le bleu du matin

Si l'heure a du couleur
c'est bleu
et s'il manque du bonheur
il y a du bleu
et s'il avait un cœur
c'est bleu
et s'il trouve des choses perdues
c'est nous

For every hour
there's a colour
and it's blue
and if there was a heart
it's blue
and if there's something to be found
it's you

how beautiful is night

Aah...
Comme c'est belle la nuit
C'est l'amour qu'elle conduit
et quand je pense a toi
Alors, c'est comme ça
je t'aime
et
voilà

Aah...
How beautiful is night
Stars guide young lovers in flight
And
darling, whenever I think of you
it's love and
it's right

*in homage to Robert Farnon

ciao ragazzi

Finitto la guerra
Di giornatti di blu
Addio la vita
Cosi breve con tu

When we're together
every day is blue
Goodbye to this life
I've shared briefly with you

etoiles

combien d'etoiles
dans le ciel
cette nuit d'amour
sont des baises pour toi

every star is a kiss
i have saved up
for tonight
with you

parlez-vous jazz?

Oui, je t'aime
ici et partout
dans ce monde
merveilleux
il y a toujours
un coin a deux

Well, yes,
here and there
everywhere
I love you
In this wonderful world
there is always
a corner for two

c'est ou le bonheur

C'est qui le roi
dans ce monde
de rêves perdus
C'est qui l'auteur
de ma vie...
Je n'aime pas l'histoire

C'est où le bonheur
les sourires
et les
fleurs

Who's the king of
this world
Who's the author
of my life...
I don't like the story

Where are the flowers
And those happy hours
I should be sharing
with you

è sempre l'italia nel mio cuore

al fine del mondo
questo mare
acqua blu
lontano di te
non fa niente
perché
è sempre
l'italia nel mio cuore

at the end of the world
by this water
clear and blue
and though
i'm away from you
it doesn't matter
because
there is always italy in my heart

non mi dimentico
le bacci
e l'occhi di più
questo grande amore
è sempre
l'italia nel mio cuore

i won't forget these kisses
your eyes
me and you
this great love
is always italy in my heart

l'amore è così

l'amore è sempre così
un avventura del cuore
non devo essere breve
perché
ogni giorno
è sempre domani
per me

in love
your heart's adventures
should never be brief
every day is always
tomorrow
for me

JAZZ IS ANOTHER LANGUAGE

Last month, a girl at the Comics A Go Go show in Vancouver (I had a table) came up & said she really liked my French poems. I also heard from my buddy Walter Zwol in Toronto that his girlfriend (who's French) likes them, too. Based on that, I figured other people must dig them too, so herewith, just about every French poem I've ever written plus a bunch of new ones. The very bilingual of you will notice two things: one being that some poems are actually in Italian & the other being that the translations are not necessarily literal. Some things, alas, just don't look or sound as nice in English. Obviously the foreign grammar & spelling is not guaranteed & if you spot a goof-up, please let me know so I can fix it for the future. There is something about French & Italian that is synonymous with romance to me. I am only sorry that I'm not more fluent in either. If you are young and angry, don't make the mistake like I did of turning your back on where you come from.

RALPH RECOMMENDS

COMBUSTIBLE EDISON, *I Swinger* (Sub Pop): If you dig Martin Denny's 50s Exotica lounge music, you'll flip over this. A little self-indulgent here & there, but otherwise cool.

LUNA, *Bewitched* (Elektra): Guest guitars by Sterling Morrison (playing exactly as he did with the Velvet Underground). Love that Velvets pop sound. The live show is not as good (get some coffee on stage boys, smile, live a little).

THE STORY OF JAMAICAN MUSIC (Island): WOW! This 4-CD box set has it all; from 1958 to 1993. Excellent liner notes. Guys like me will quibble over the track selection; the 75-81 disc is especially brilliant.

BACKBEAT (Virgin): There are 2 CDs of movie music; one has the rock songs (an excellent party CD - but way too short - keep it on repeat all night), & the other has jazz music but more importantly, the first ever look at the paintings of Stu Sutcliffe. Total 50s Beat art. He's been neglected too long.

CHRIS WILSON & THE SNEETCHES (Marilyn): A neat little EP from ex-Flamin' Groovies singer/guitarist. Extremely rough around the edges, but plenty of jangly Byrds 12-string for all. Roy Loney even joins in on some live Groovies tracks. I like "Never Love Again" the best (of course). Chris aims high, falls short, & God bless him for trying.

PENELOPE HOUSTON, The Whole Wide World (Heydey): "Glad I'm A Girl" is a great anthem. Her songwriting is on the unplugged side of Tori Amos & Sarah McLachlan. This one seems to have slipped through the cracks. Worth your while to track down. Also great are "Sweetheart" & "Maybe Love".

On that note, one of the guilty pleasures of working at Nettwerk is getting tickets to see Sarah McLachlan in concert. I always get inspired & I always walk out wanting to do a good deed; there's so much warmth between the stage & audience. See and hear for yourself. She's still on tour. She'll be in Europe in October. If you have a modem, some of my artwork & comments on the music biz are available on the Nettwerk BBS, 604-731-7007. No charge to join. Download all you want.

Speaking of tickets, I will soon be locked out of Veda Hille's concerts for bumbling up her address last month (it's the ink fumes). Send $20 (includes postage) for her cool CD to Veda herself at: Ball Of Flame Productions, 3126 W. 13th Ave., Vancouver, BC, Canada, V6K 2V3.

RALPH L'ARTISTE?

It's true. I used the best of 90s software to create a digital art piece that (surprise) looks just like a cool 50s movie poster! My tribute to cult director Ed Wood is available as a full page in the April/May issue of MEDIA WEST, 300-1497 Marine Dr., West Vancouver, BC, Canada, V7T 1B8. Send them $5 for a copy. It will also be blown up to poster size in a limited edition of 75 as part of The Pixel Pushers digital art show on Granville Island, Vancouver, in June. Numbered & signed par moi, these posters are available from MEDIA WEST at, I think, $300 each (yikes!). Write them for more details. Hmm...now where'd I put my beret? I feel a still life coming on...hey that loaf of bread looks tasty....

COVER ILLUSTRATION

A pencil sketch by Michael W. Kaluta, who, along with Berni Wrightson, Jeff Jones & Howard Chaykin, brought classical romanticism to mainstream comic books in the early 70s. His work on the DC **Shadow** books was particularly awesome. This sketch was given to me at a 1973 Detroit Comic Convention & has been buried away until now when it seems aptly appropriate to this issue's foreign adventures. There is a **Shadow** movie coming this summer & I wouldn't be surprised if they borrow heavily from Mr. Kaluta's definitive visual interpretation. Twenty years ago when I was a snotty little comic fan, Mike Kaluta was a pretty cool guy. I assume he still is.

RALPH is published monthly. Written & silk screened one page at a time on 1950s Gestetner duplicating machines by RALPH ALFONSO. Correspondence to: RALPH, Box 505 - 1288 Broughton St., Vancouver, BC, CANADA, V6G 2B5. My e.mail address is: ralpha6982@aol.com. My design skills are for hire. Business calls only to: 604-654-2929 or FAX: 604-654-1993 (both are work numbers). **THIS IS A LIMITED EDITION PRINTING OF:** 2500 (lots, eh?). ©1994 by Ralph Alfonso. Distributed by hand or by mail to cool people and places all over. I'll mail you a copy every month if you send me 12 Canadian stamps or monetary equivalent ($5 in the USA & 12 x IRCs outside North America). Back issues are $1.00 each. My cassette is $3.00.

LOOKING FOR THE MABUHAY GARDENS

The last time I was in San Francisco, I woke up in a smelly tour bus with a heavy metal band; parked outside the front door of the Stone club on Broadway. I didn't realize it then, but I was right across the street from what used to be the Mabuhay Gardens. The Mabuhay was where punk met San Francisco, thanks to promoter Dirk Dirksen. Bands like Crime, Avengers, Screamers & zines like *Search and Destroy*. 1979; I sent my band, The Diodes, to the Mabuhay. The west coast scene fascinated us & even tho The Diodes made it to the coast well past the '77 prime; it was still personally a big deal.

The SF punk era is detailed in two books; *California Hardcore*, and *Punk '77*...both equally fascinating. The Toronto scene, alas, is still unchronicled. If you have my old *New York Rocker* articles, you can staple them together & call it a book (hmmm......).

San Francisco is where the Sex Pistols played their final gig...geez, what's with this place, everybody plays their final gigs here.

It's cool how some of that original '77 vibrancy is manifesting again with the new sense of indie community.

On another level, for guys like myself, sometimes I feel on the outside looking in; watching something I helped get started now another layer in the mainstream. Maybe I liked it better when "alternative" was just another word in the dictionary. The other thing is, with all these marketing robots trying to woo the 'generation x' demographic (I also liked it better when this was a good band that Billy Idol sang in, thanks very much. It was also a great 60s youth gone bad paperback before that.); what about all us 30-something ex-punks? We even get to lose out on being marketed to. *sigh*

Anyway, so now it's 1994. The Mabuhay is just another building at 443 Broadway. I finally get to see it 17 years too late. Kind of like when I made it to the ruins of the Star Club in Hamburg, 1986. You're hoping to get a sense of history, some kind of spirit force leaping out of the ground...but really, it's just a bunch of bricks. Broadway itself is full of crappy nude joints with ugly people outside asking you to check them out nude inside.

Baby when that snare drum hits
Baby that's when you shake your hips
and Baby when that hi-hat slips
Baby that's when you start to strip
and Baby when those lights go out
Baby that's when you make me shout

FAMOUS FOR 15 PAGES

Went to a poetry reading. Saw Jennifer Joseph read & she also runs a publishing company, MANIC D PRESS. Get her great *Poet's Guide to San Francisco* ($2) & ask for a catalog at the same time; Box 410804, San Francisco, Ca, USA, 94141.

If you are perhaps a creature neither male nor female, black fingernails, white vampyre flesh, black lipstick, candles everywhere, perhaps an exotic pet (snake?) etc. etc. (Yes, I know all about it. We've gone out - I managed to escape!) ....then you'll love Danielle Willis. There's a great interview with her in FIZ #11. She's just as cool in performance. There are two books; *Corpse Delectable* ($4) and *Dogs In Lingerie* ($5.95). This is intense stuff, so beware if reality offends you. Send $$ to: Zeitgeist Press, 4368 Piedmont Ave., Oakland, CA, 94611.

David West had a cocktail pianist accompany his reminisces of bad bars, sad drag queens and low-end hipsters. I really liked his style. He has two books; *Elegy For The Old Stud* ($6, Manic D Press), and *BAR* ($3, Zeitgeist).

John Giorno was the headliner. His new book is *You've Got To Burn To Shine*. His sexual liaisons with Warhol, Keith Haring et al are fairly explicit (and then some!).

Man, next to all these guys, my life just

feels ...er...well...Canadian. The current indie publishing phenomenon where anyone can be in print for 15 pages is almost 100% personal diary in nature, be it comics, poetry, fiction, etc. Being a real life older brother, I just feel like saying hey, c'mon, it's not all that bad, but at the same time being the older brother that's let everyone down, I look at myself pushing the broom behind life's parade & while it's not any better than what you've got, actually things really aren't that bad....at least I get to keep all the cool stuff society leaves behind.

Hung around the North Beach area where the original Beats gathered. City Lights Bookstore is a cool stop. You can't leave without buying something. The Vesuvio Bar next door is ok, but if you really want to be depressed, head over to Spec's across the street. It'll totally ruin your trip and have you writing about it for a good month thereafter.

Lit a candle at the Church of St. Peter and St. Paul at Washington Square. Whatever your inclinations; a cool meditative stop in the middle of the day. Nobody around. Just you and ... Him/Her/ It/ Whatever.

Another good spot is the roof of The San Francisco Art Institute (on Chestnutt, just up the street from Tower Records). Incredible views of the city plus a cheap student cafe. Beware, when you first come into the college...lots and lots of harsh student paintings & sculptures on the human condition of hopelessness & despair...lots & lots of it...so much it'll have you reeling at the realization that life in general probably sucks...whew!... you'll have to sit down for a sec in the beautiful courtyard & come to grips with this. And you know what? Life ain't bad...but this art is! Had me going for a minute there....

HAIGHT ASHBURY

Best sight was a homeless guy who's probably been on the same corner since the 50s, giving advice to a young beggar next to him, Everybody's gotta start somewhere..."

WELL, I JOINED THE HUMAN RACE AND I LOST

Well, I joined the human race
but I lost
I tried to find my place
but I got lost
I tried to make a stand
but I fell off
I tried to make a point
but it got soft
Well, I really tried to SHOUT
but
I got a cough...

(*Hey, if you've got a line that fits send it in)

RALPH RECOMMENDS:

DaDaBaby, 382 E. 4th St., North Vancouver, BC, V7L 1J2. Edited by jazz musician/poet Jamie Reid, this cool pamphlet is free but send money for postage. Guaranteed to make you scratch your head.

WATER ROW BOOKS, Catalog #62. A mail-order catalog of virtually every Beat & Cool related book you could ever possibly want. It's free from; Box 438, Sudbury, MA, USA, 01776 or fax 508-229-0885.

WOW!, 155-2496 E. Hastings, Vancouver, BC, V5K 1Z1. Your basic xeroxed, pasted-up crooked-looking fanzine except this is the best so far with more than you would ever want to know about the Vancouver indie music/zine scene. Send editor Jody (no last name) $1.50. Sorry my ex-Toronto friends, but Vancouver is what's happening. Read this & weep ...but don't move here!

SLAPSHOTS, c/o Pals Restaurant, St. Andrews Shopping Center, Yonge & Orchard Heights Blvd, Aurora, Ont., L4G 3W3. If you are ever in Aurora, visit my old boss Tom Williams at his PALS restaurant. Tell him I sent you & maybe he'll kick you out! But, you gotta get this totally hilarious newsletter with pix of Vera Lynn (for real) hanging out at PALS & all sorts of stuff too ridiculous to be believed. If you want to know what Canada is all about, this is where you start. The newsletter is free. Oh yeah, Tom & I both worked at ATTIC Records. Don't ask him about how I broke the elevator on moving day....

KNUCKLE SANDWICH, 998 S. Thompson Rd., Suite 15, Lafayette, CA, 94549. $3. Hard-boiled detectives, babes & 40s-50s-o-rama. New fiction & wild old magazine/movie clippings. For the Vegas man.

HOLY TITCLAMPS, Box 591275, San Francisco, CA, 94159-1275. $3. In addition to some pretty good writing, this gay zine has the most comprehensive listing of queer zines worldwide. Music reviews & more.

SO I JOINED THE HUMAN RACE AND I LOST

This issue is mostly thoughts on my trip to San Francisco (the poetry it inspired next issue). It's interesting how the original beats ran away from the spotlight & like animals in the wild, froze still, and got run over. Now, the new breed not only welcomes the media but actively cultivate and exploit it. These are exciting times for poetry, even if the world at large could care less.

RALPH RECOMMENDS SOME MORE

WOW COOL, Winter '94 Catalog. 48 Shattuck Square, #149, Berkeley, CA, 94704. Distributors of cool small press comics from all across the USA

CAMEO, 303-102 25th Ave. SW, Calgary, Alberta, T2S 1K9. $2. This is so slick & cool, I'd already bought it before I realized it was from...Calgary! The next cool Canadian city & I'm actually going to go there in August & check it out! I like the music, photography & graphics coming out of Calgary these days...it's a long ways from the Ten Foot Henry's club. Did I mention the time I did lights one night for the Ripchords? Where are The Ripchords?

PROBE, c/o Aaron Muentz, Box 5068, Pleasanton, CA, 94566. $6. An incredible indie music zine with tons of reviews, articles, interviews & nude pictures of the editor's girlfriends, his contributors, his friends' girlfriends, bands......What? All I know is, it works. Issue #3 comes with two free 7" singles (5 groups!)

GEARHEAD #2, Box 421219, San Francisco, CA, 94142-1219. $7. Cars. Girls. Cars. Biker movies. Hot Rods. Custom Cars. Peter Bagge cover. Indie reviews. Total Americana low-brow. Free 7" w/Red Aunts/Clawhammer. A whopping 116 pages!!!

ART COM, Box 193123 Rincon Annex, San Francisco, CA, 94119-3123. Art Com is a cultural organization specializing in the interface of contemporary art & new communication technology. This is a free catalog of incredible videos they have for sale: poetry, industrial culture, music, video art, etc. Now, the avant garde right in your living room!

PUPPY TOSS, Box 9849, Berkeley, CA, USA, 94709. Puppy Toss is an artists' collective who release amazing indie comics and art stuff. Write them for a catalog. I recommend their collective comic, SKIM LIZARD #2 ($1.50).

As usual, tell these people I sent you.

MALCOLM McLAREN, *Paris* (BMG); Brilliant. Leave it to Malcolm to out-French the French. It has the first song Francoise Hardy has sung in English in 25 years! Photos by Jean Baptiste Mondino! Plus spoken word by Catherine Deneuve. He does an admirable job of trying to distill everything that was jazzy cool about Paris in the early 60s & what it meant to him as an English art student. Too smart for most, this will be our private pleasure until Madonna rips him off again.

BLOSSOM DEARIE (Verve). To set the mood, buy Blossom's two currently re-issued CDs. When she recorded these sessions in 1959, Blossom Dearie had already spent most of the 50s playing Paris nightclubs. Smoky, jazzy, swinging. This is the real thing. Accept no 90s substitutes.

ANITA O'DAY (Verve). Tired of Ella & Billie? Discover Anita. She totally swings and has a great voice!

PEGGY LEE, *Latin Ala Lee* (Capitol). I don't know if this is on CD, but you always see the vinyl cheap at garage sales, so I finally got one. WOW! Incredible Latin tinged versions of stuff you know.

COVER ILLUSTRATION

I actually drew this myself without any help from a computer. Don't tell anyone.

CHICAGO PEACE & MUSIC FESTIVAL AUG 6-7, CRICKET HILL, INFO CALL BILL: 312-252-9150

RALPH is published monthly. Written & silk screened one page at a time on 1950s Gestetner duplicating machines by RALPH ALFONSO. Correspondence to: RALPH, Box 505 - 1288 Broughton St., Vancouver, BC, CANADA, V6G 2B5. My e.mail address is: ralpha6982@aol.com. My design skills are for hire. Business calls only to: 604-654-2929 or FAX: 604-654-1993 (both are work numbers). **THIS IS A LIMITED EDITION PRINTING OF:** 2800 (wow!). ©1994 by Ralph Alfonso. Distributed by hand or by mail to cool people and places all over. I'll mail you a copy every month if you send me 12 Canadian stamps or monetary equivalent ($5 in the USA & 12 x IRCs outside North America). Back issues are $1.00 each. My cassette is $3.00.

FREE   No. 20! 1994

RALPH

COFFEE, JAZZ, & POETRY

Goatee Nation

WE'RE THE PEOPLE THAT LOVE FORGOT

Baby,
We're the people that love
Forgot
We're the presents that
No one got
We're whatever you never
Gave a second thought
Well,
We're happy
I guess we're not
We're the last car
In the parking lot
We're whatever's cold
When you want hot
We're a blur in the picture
You just shot
We're the people that love
Forgot
Well,
We're happy
I guess we're not

HEY WHATEVER

Fire your canons
Let the words fly
Straight to my heart
Baby, say what you will
I love you still

Burn my letters
Cut out my picture
Re-write the book but
Baby, say what you will
I love you still

MADELINE KNOWS HOW

Madeline knows how
And I love her so
now
But please don't you
Tell her
Or she'll turn
all red
And want to know
Everything I've said

JAZZ WEST COAST

I can't say much
When we're kissing
But I sure can smell
Your sweetness
With the wind blowing through
This cable car for two
There's probably a whole world
Around us
But we can't see much
With our eyes closed
Enjoying the warmth
Of me holding you
Our lips share a moment
But we share a lifetime
Together
In love

SOMEWHERE AT THE END

Sleeping in this nowhere car
outside the motel
we can't afford to get into
This wretched life
And if I'm sinking
Well at least
There's an angel
With me all the way

We may be laughing
But it won't feed this hunger
And it doesn't matter
Just keep driving...
Somewhere at the end
Is the beginning

THIS CHILD OF MINE

This child of mine
That I hold
Close to my heart
And from the cold
You're everything this world could be
You're everything in this world to me

(with love for John & Sheryll -
the world's coolest couple
now the world's coolest parents)

I WON'T BE SO LUCKY

I want more
Than you're willing to give me
I want to know that
You've got a heart
But I won't be so lucky

GLORIA DRANK DIRTY WATER ON HER WAY TO THE 99TH FLOOR

Gloria drank dirty water
on her way to the 99th floor
There was Long Tall Sally
and Lola, too
They were having some drinks
Well, maybe quite a few
They were waiting for Eddie
It was getting late
The elevator was locked
So he was climbing the stairs
And when he got to the top
Well, he was too tired to rock

MY WONDERFUL GOATEE

My wonderful goatee
I'm proud to have it
It's a prized possession
And I wear it well

IT'S YOUR WORLD NOW

I still look the same
I guess I'll never change
But the world has spun
much faster
And it's probably thrown me off
Because I don't know what
you're saying
And I know that for you
It's just the same
I'm trying to make you understand me
But I don't know how
Well, it's just no use
It's your world now

THE ENGLISH LANGUAGE

The English language
is great
but
sometimes
the words fail me

I LOVE YOU BABY BUT YOU GOTTA STOP WEARING THOSE UGLY SHOES

I love you baby,
but
you gotta stop wearing
those ugly shoes
Now I would normally
never complain
but
they must
cause you some pain

WELL I MAY BE UGLY BUT AT LEAST I'M SMART

Well, I may be ugly
But at least I'm smart
When you come looking for a job
Maybe I'll give you a start

AND SO

And so...
Into the night
Onto the highway
Through the mountains
Under the bridges
Around the corners
And into the valley

Letting life blur
While I am with you

A NOTE ON "GLORIA": I don't mean to be obscure, but this has references to songs by Them, The Standells, The Moving Sidewalks, Little Richard, The Kinks, and Eddie Cochran., who by the way was born Oct. 3, 1938. Le Rock C'est Ca, Baby.

GOATEES FOR EVERYONE! (GOATEE NATION™)

Thousands of goateed, striped shirt poets hunched over whirling Gestetner machines - sparkling sheets of emotion flying out in all directions! *Sigh* It brings a tear to my eye. Despite my inadvertedly romanticizing the Gestetner back from obscurity, this image could only have been possible with the original Beats. While that 2nd-hand machine may look tempting, don't buy it! You will also need a drum stencil-cutter & previous experience. Plus BAD NEWS: supplies were longago discontinued and once existing stocks disappear, it's over for me (unless YOU have a basement full of ink). I've had this machine since I was probably 15...I guess it's a little too late to get a life now.

GOATEE NAIVETE

I've certainly had my share of bad haircuts over the years & now I can proudly add a bad goatee to the collection. How is this possible? There are more goatees per sq. foot than there used to be bolo ties. I get more weird people bugging me now than when I had a cute Brian Jones mop top. I guess I just want to be anti-cute for a while. A very old friend called me up & asked if I could possibly be as naive as my poetry implied or is it all ironic, perhaps with deeper sub-text? Whoa, I'm certainly not that clever, in fact, I'm so naive, when I helped my last girlfriend move out of our apartment, I asked, "Hey, does this mean we've broken up?"

OH YEAH, THE POEMS

This collection was inspired prior, during & after my visit to San Francisco, mecca of Goatee Nation™. The outsider observing from the inside is how I've always felt, altho you can't hang back & watch your relationships happen - you sort of have to participate, unfortunately. You can't live and watch your own movie, too. Hey, I've just discovered that my work is passed around in classrooms in Saskatoon and Ajax - which fills me with a sense of responsibility all of a sudden. As a possible role model for Canadian youth, I say - there's a whole world outside your room, open the window & have a look for a second.

RALPH RECOMMENDS

JALE, *Dreamcake* (Sub Pop). This all-girl jangly rock group from *Halifax* (a good town to get piss drunk in-trust me) sent me their CD plus cool stickers. My favorite song is "Mend" because it's probably a good song to smooch to. They're the only band that ever sent me anything, so they get top spot here. Hey, speaking of *Halifax*, I just designed the Sloan concert posters for their Western tour, what does this all mean? Who will send me PAL-O-MINE chocolate bars (world's best candy - only available in the Maritimes)?

OBSCURE, Box 1334, Milwaukee, WI, USA, 53201, $2, is an amazing cool publication that reprints the best bits of other fanzines. Beautifully assembled & written.

.TIFF, Box 97011, 149 Roncesvalle Ave., Toronto, Ont., M6R 3B3, Free, 56 newsprint pages of reviews, slacker stuff, lo-tech, coffee, internet stuff, big words & nice layout.

CAFFEINE NATION QUARTERLY, 4024 W. 20th St., Vancouver, BC, V6S 1G5, $2, anything & everything to do with coffee. Cool coffee clippings, reviews, theories, etc.

BUNYON, c/o Robert Dayton, 317-A Cambie St., Vancouver, BC, V6B 2N4, $2. Interviews, comix, reviews & Robert's very personal journal plus Catholic recollections!

BACK OF A CAR, #4636 MPO, Vancouver, BC, V6B 4A1, $3. Judith Beeman's very slick Big Star zine plus comix, reviews, Alex Chilton, Big Star, and..er..Big Star.

This issue's paper & ink costs plus $400 postage bill is courtesy of my hard work designing CD covers for: BIF NAKED, PURE, ALYSSA NIELSEN, ANNIHILATOR, THRILL SQUAD, THE GRAPES OF WRATH (hits comp), RYMES WITH ORANGE, & cool posters for Perryscope. Thank you to STRATHCONA BOOKS in Edmonton for your kind donation. Please visit this store.

COVER ILLUSTRATION

Several issues ago, I off-handedly made a remark about The Goatee Nation™ & the tag seems to have struck a chord with people which kind of frightens me, so I called up Calgary's own Tom Bagley & begged him to immediately put it in its proper context. Tom or "Tomb" is for sure Canada's coolest cartoonist & as always, he is for hire (he lettered the logo on the PURE CD cover I just designed). He is at 403-284-3504.

RALPH is published monthly. Written & silk screened one page at a time on 1950s Gestetner duplicating machines by RALPH ALFONSO. Correspondence to: RALPH, Box 505 - 1288 Broughton St., Vancouver, BC, CANADA, V6G 2B5. My e.mail address is: ralpha6982@aol.com. My design skills are for hire. TEL: 604-654-2929 or FAX: 604-654-1993 (be cool, both are work numbers). **THIS IS A LIMITED EDITION PRINTING OF:** 2800 (Canada's best read unknown poet). ©1994 by Ralph Alfonso. Distributed by hand or by mail to cool people and places all over. I'll mail you a copy every month if you send me 12 Canadian stamps or $$$ equivalent ($5 in the USA & 12 x IRCs outside North America). Back issues are $1.00 each. My cassette is $3.00.

OUR LITTLE RENDEZVOUS

It's half past midnight
Baby, are you still there
We got Chuck on the radio
Up on the roof
Cause we're twistin' there

We got the BBQ goin'
And the neighbours
They don't care
Cause we're drinkin' pop
and dancin'
In the midnight air

And when we stopped
To rest up in a chair
We looked out and saw
All across this city fair
On every roof
From here to there
People dancing everywhere

*With love for newlyweds Dave & Jan
The music may stop but Chuck Berry is still on top!

BRIGHTON MIST

Yeah
Bang that gong
J. Arthur Rank
The mist of Brighton
Is rolling across the pier
And we are here
Revving up the engine
On this beach with no sand
We kiss
You hold my hand
I love you
Parkas flying in the wind
Vespa shining in
The morning sun
Stevie's on the radio
ShaLaLaLaLee
Baby
You and me
In this England
We are free

OO LA LA C'EST COMME CA

Oo la là
c'est comme ca
Baises
Bons Bons
Chocolats
Toutes ces choses
Et voila
Oui, je t'aime
C'est comme ca

Oo la là
It's like this
Kisses
Bons Bons
and
Chocolits

LE MONDE C'EST FAIT EN RONDE

Le monde
C'est fait
en ronde
et
en avant
avec toi
ma blonde
ici
dans l'univers
c'est a nous
chaque etoile
un coeur
je te donne

*I can't even begin to translate this,
except to say it's about being in love,
flying out into space on your own planet,
and every star is a heart you can give.
What?

WHERE ARE THE BUMPER BOATS IN SALMON ARM, BC, BABY

Where are the Bumper Boats
in Salmon Arm, BC, baby
Why is nobody downtown
On a Sunday
Are we going to sleep by the
banks of the beautiful
Shuswap Lake, can
you even pronounce it
Or are we stopping for fries at the mall
At the end of the street
Kelowna or Kamloops
Where would you rather go?
What's with this one lane highway
I'm going too slow
Don't smoke the last cigarette
Wait till we get to Vernon

C'EST YEH YEH OU OUAIS OUAIS

C'est
Yeh Yeh
ou
Ouais Ouais
N'importe quoi
Je le sais

41 GREAT WINDMILL ST.

There is no one here
When I'm dancing with you
I can only hear music
Just meant for two

SEPTEMBER TRAVELS

For the hell of it, I drove 12 hours (YAY! The Rockies!) either way to Calgary, Alberta, my new favorite city. Can people be any nicer?

For example, I ran into Rich E., most excellent drummer for HUEVOS RANCHEROS, and he was genuinely hurt that I didn't tell him I was coming to town. "You could've stayed over at my place," he offered. "It's a big house, and I GOT BACON!" How more Canadian can one guy be than to offer from his private trove of most treasured bacon! I tried very hard to hide my tears. God, I love this land!

I drank like a fish at the very cool Ship & Anchor pub with Ian Chiclo, editor of VOX magazine ($2 from 127 MacEwan Hall, Univ of Calgary, AB, T2N 1N4. The bible of the Calgary music scene) and host of a very RALPH-like radio show on CJSW Radio - Coffee, Jazz & Chet!).

And how amazing is Tom Bagley, King of Kartoons? We prowled through the great used book & record stores (love those George Shearing latin lps!) & hit jackpot at the secret movie poster warehouse where I wandered out with more than I'll ever want on my all time fave rock movie, PRIVILEGE. He and wife Colette even invited me out to his brother's cool BBQ where we had a Chuck Berry style outdoor cookout. Tom's secret life is as lead ghoul of THE FORBIDDEN DIMENSION (buy ALL their CDs and singles!).

BAND ALERT: CHIXDIGGIT - guitar pop punk.

And THEN....I flew to Toronto for a weekend to see my good pal Dave MacMillan get hitched to the lovely Jan Crabtree. A tip of the Berry Beret to the excellent Jack DeKeyzer whose band smoked through a great set of 50s rock that kept yours truly dancing all night! I had no time to visit my ex-friends so apologies to all, but I was so bummed out by the excess of Queen St., my old neighbourhood, that I just spent all day Sunday drinking at the Black Bull pub with ex-Diodes drummer John Hamilton (we hadn't seen each other in possibly 14 years) and good pal, photographer Tom Robe. There is a lot of Toronto punk history between the three of us.   In another issue: LOOKING FOR THE CRASH 'N' BURN. Clue: It's at the corner of Duncan & Pearl.

OO LA LA! BAISES, BONS BONS ET CHOCOLATS

Yum. Yum. My unrelenting love for the England and France that no longer exist manifests itself again. I honestly can't explain it, except either I must've been someone cool in a previous life or it could be the insularity of the French and British cultures of Montreal in the early 60s where I grew up, before the impending global village made everyone the same everywhere. It's funny to me how you may be someone who's possibly spending the 90s discovering the 70s and how I, in turn, spent most of the 70s discovering the 60s, thereby spending the 80s simultaneously trying to catch up on the 70s and trying to keep my hair up with as much gel and hairspray as possible, leaving me with the 90s still trying to get that gunk out.

COVER ILLUSTRATION

Ah yes, the elusive Beatnik Chick, the Holy Grail of smelly male Beats since the 50s. Trust me, they don't exist. I only saw one once, when I was possibly 8 years old, at the corner of Melrose and Upper Lachine in Montreal, outside the greasy diner that is now an Italian bakery (best tomato foccacio pizza I've ever tasted, sorry San Francisco). I remember being profoundly awed, having never seen anyone like that before (or since). Having said all that, it's inevitable that you may refute all this. Well, I don't want to hear about it. I'll only feel depressed.

Our cover this month is by the ultra-cool Miss Molly Kiely, whose work has appeared in ANSWER ME, SHLOCK, EVIL®, APOLOGY, but is perhaps best known for her comic book, DIARY OF A DOMINATRIX (Eros/Fantagraphics). Miss Kiely currently lives in San Francisco and is (surprise!) a former Canadian who misses "President's Choice" products. Molly is available as a free-lance illustrator for cool projects, 415-771-1789.

RALPH RECOMMENDS

CHUCK BERRY, *St. Louis To Liverpool; Back Home*(Chess/MCA). After all is said and done, it all comes back to Chuck. I recently dusted off these two lps for old times' sake, and rediscovered Mr. Berry all over again. The first lp was released shortly after he came out of prison (the 1st time) and the latter was his return to Chess after a sad sojourn to Mercury Records. Chuck Berry was literally the first beat poet (check out his snazzy beret on the back of the *St. Louis* lp). Mixing souped up jazz, latin and jump rhythms, Chuck gave away the blueprint that lesser lights have since plonked their skyscrapers onto. Lyrically, he championed the innocent idealism of young love, shading it occasionally with a nod and longing for a kind of cosmopolitan French sophistication that had long held an attraction for most jazz musicians of the day since the 40s. Hmm...sound familiar? Just know this: whatever it is that any current snotty know-it-alls are trying to say - Chuck could say in half the time and half the words.

CAFFEINE, Box 4231-306, Woodland Hills, Ca, USA, 91365. $5 for a sample. Absolutely fantastic 72-pg slick mag of poetry, fiction, reviews and way more. Your eyes will pop out of your head.

LIVEWIRE, 4337 Percival Ave, Burnaby, BC, V5G 3S4. $2. Huevos/Shadowy Men fans wanting to connect with the roots of rock instrumental music, this is the place. How cool is this zine? The Huevos are subscribers & letter writers! The twang's the thang!

Poets/Writers: Submit your work to: THE MUSE JOURNAL, 226 Lisgar St., Toronto, Ont., M6J 3G7. Sample issue is $4.50 for a good overview of the Toronto scene. THE SKINNY, 57 Medford St., Kitchener, Ont., N2M 2C9. Sample issue is $2. An earnest little publication.

COMETBUS #32, an incredible 52-page personal diary beautifully hand-lettered. Is it fact or fiction. Both? Who cares. Once you start reading, you can't stop. Available for $2 from Wow Cool Mail Order, 48 Shattuck Sq, Box 149, Berkeley, CA, USA, 94704.

OUT OF BOUNDS, Box 4809, Alexandria, VA, 22303. $3.50 for a 76 page zine with a politicized slant but lots of reviews and cartoons to offset it. They are also a record label.

JELLYBEAN ZINE, 113 Fleetwood Ln, Minoa, NY, USA, 13116. $2 for over 50 pages of general indie rock photocopier everything. Tons of zine & music reviews.

HELP ME KEEP MY FANZINE GOING! IF YOU DONATE $10 OR MORE, I WILL SEND YOU A ONE YEAR SUBSCRIPTION PLUS A FREE DONOVAN CD I DESIGNED FOR NETTWERK.

RALPH is published monthly. Written & silk screened one page at a time on 1950s Gestetner duplicating machines by RALPH ALFONSO. Correspondence to: RALPH, Box 505 - 1288 Broughton St., Vancouver, BC, CANADA, V6G 2B5. My e.mail address is: ralpha6982@aol.com. My design skills are for hire. TEL: 604-654-2929 or FAX: 604-654-1993 (be cool, both are work numbers). **THIS IS A LIMITED EDITION PRINTING OF:** 2800 (where do they go?). ©1994 by Ralph Alfonso. Distributed by hand or by mail to cool people and places all over. I'll mail you a copy every month if you send me 12 Canadian stamps or $$$ equivalent ($5 in the USA & 12 x IRCs outside North America). Back issues are $1.00 each. My cassette is $3.00.

FREE No. 22, Nov. 1994

RALPH

COFFEE, JAZZ, & POETRY

THE GARGOYLES COME DOWN FROM THE CATHEDRAL AT NIGHT

THE GARGOYLES COME DOWN FROM THE CATHEDRAL AT NIGHT

The gargoyles come down
from The Cathedral
at night
I know
I saw them at the cafe
on the corner
Pierre was the oldest one
He said it was ok
if I sat at their table
"We really don't get going
until midnight." he said,
"So we like to have a little cup
and a croissant first.
Sometimes the angels will join us
but their shift is more from
dawn till dusk."
Jean-Francois was the smallest one
and Serge was the tallest
Sometimes they amuse themselves
with what each has seen over the years
and sometimes Pierre will light
a cigarette and that means that
several points of arcane theology
will be discussed.
The Cathedral Bells ring midnight
and the gargoyles stretch
their arms back and prepare to climb
to their posts
Serge smiles at me,
"Now you be good," he says,
and winks
and pats me on the back,
"I'll be watching you."

50 STEPHANIE ST.

All things considered
I guess I'm doing fine
No need to be angry
It's your problem
If you're gone
I can stand here
In this empty room
And be thankful it's all mine

THE LAST KNIGHT LEFT AT THE ROUND TABLE

I am proud to bear your ideal
I will be the soldier for your faith
While some may
Embrace sadness and
Forget the Quest
Lost hope will always be my guest
I will be the smile
You have worked hard to forget
I am the heart that will not rust
I will keep it pure for all of us
We have been shunned
and forgotten
Accustomed to the darkness
That has hampered this long journey
Let me be the child
You have long since sent away
Let me lift the sword
to sparkle on The Holy Grail
Let me be the one to see
your heart
Let me be the strength
that will not fail

BABY WHEN PETER PERRETT SINGS I GO TO HEAVEN ON SILVER WINGS

Baby when Peter Perrett sings
I go to heaven on silver wings
And when these stars are out at night
He just makes me
Want to hold on tight
To all of you
With all my might

THE MUSIC IS ON MY SIDE

If nothing else
The music is on my side
If nothing else
It's my bridge
Across this great divide
When no one cared
I nurtured it
By my side
You've got the house
But I still live inside

YOU LIGHT THE CANDLES WHILE THE ANGELS LOOK DOWN

You light the candles
While the angels look down
from your walls
You shed your many layers
of black
and nothing is ever said
except for the anger
in this bed
Your dark fingernails
dig in
to hold on to
me
In your world of
ice and darkness
I am the warmth
that lights your heart
When you sleep
I smell the perfume in
your ice white hair
You've drawn me in
and it's my hope
to draw you out

WE WERE SO PRETTY WHEN

We were so pretty when
Everything was working then
Planes stayed up in the sky
You always laughed
Never cried
Well, things never go to plan
Sitting here
Watching bridges span
Our worlds
All we knew is left in our eyes
Everything else
A sad surprise

We can never close the book
We always want to have a look
When we were so pretty when

INVISIBLE DOMINION

In the kingdom of our sleep
where
each day returns as
the sum of uneven parts
and insignificant minutiae
suddenly become masters
of the realm
where worlds crumble
at the flutter of an eyelid
on this tentative landscape
our life is re-constructed
without flaw and imperfection
every stumble and fall
is now
triumph and achievement

THERE ARE SO MANY COLOURS BUT YOU ARE THE BRIGHTEST OF THEM ALL

I love you most of all
In the glory that is Fall
Tell me
Who can resist
To hold your hand
To share a kiss

MINE IS THE LAST PRAYER GOD HEARS EVERY NIGHT

I sweep the church floors
After everyone's left
I put the hymnals back in their place
I am the little curly-haired man
You never see my face
Mine is the last candle
That is lit here at night
Mine is the last prayer
God hears every night

*for my dad

REMEMBER PETER PERRETT: The lead singer of UK group THE ONLY ONES was the one true romantic in the midst of 70s punk; his haunting cries lost in the din. It's unfortunate they will only ever be remembered for "Another Girl, Another Planet," & some dodgy live CDs. The best lp is BABY'S GOT A GUN (Epic) & not available on CD. Find it. Buy it.

INTERVIEW WITH THE BEATNIK

The theme this month is Gothic, I guess. A certain sadness, but also hope. Being Italian, I was brought up accepting sadness as an everyday part of living. When you're Latin, it's quite a point of honour at dinner as to how tragic your day has been thus far. It makes each happiness that much more of a victory. Triumph or defeat isn't as important as how you deal with it.

COVER PHOTOGRAPH

My old friend Diana at the top of Notre Dame Cathedral in her favourite city, Paris, in 1983. Sadly, this is the only photograph I have left from our friendship. Gargoyle Jean-Francois is in the background. Yours truly is behind the camera.

OH NO! RALPH SELLS OUT! BEATNIK LITE™

What an October! I was interviewed by Peter Gzowski for MORNINGSIDE, airing nationally Oct. 3 on CBC Radio. I blathered for 27 minutes, completely unheard of for an obscure guy like myself, thanks to producer Mary Lynk's refusal to edit the pre-recorded piece as she really liked how it sounded. Judging by the cascade of mail (200+ letters!), so did a lot of you. From the comments, it seems my laugh was quite popular, my attitude, & oh yeah, the poetry, too (thank God!). Not to let it all go to my head, I also got a call from my mom with a brief lecture on money management. Joining me for the broadcast were guitarist Michael Rummen & my pal Tom Harrison on scat vocals/bongos/percussion. We had such a blast, that I volunteered our services for the Nettwerk Records Annual BBQ; my first ever public performance, closing the show after GINGER and ITCH (shameless plugs here). Drummer Paul Brennan had a compulsion to leave the audience & join us on stage, becoming the fourth "Ralph". I was shocked to read a good review of my "set" since the only thing I remember of my time on stage was that my left leg was freaking out & I had lost control over it. Next thing you know, the 4 of us are being taped for CBC-TV's ZERO AVENUE (this time I sat on a high stool in case my leg wandered off again). I had honestly believed my stuff would never work as spoken word, but matching some poems to specific musical patterns seems to work. The TV experience was so good, we decided to have fun & maybe make a little money, too. Despite all this acclaim, I still seem to be as poor as ever. Hmmm, maybe the French will discover me & fly us over (they've got some good food there).

GOATEE TO GO! RALPH ON TOUR!

I've teamed up with my pals THE VAN PELT TRIO for an exciting double-bill of Julie London meets Jack Kerouac for drinks in a bad bar ambience. Dig out the elbow-patch jackets, slip into some black & come down for good fun, good jazz, & unfortunately, me, too (you'll live).

NOV. 24, MALCOLM LOWRY ROOM, Vancouver, 4125 E. Hastings, 685-0143, FREE
Room honcho & cool author Michael Turner has promised to bring in really good coffee for the night in addition to wearing an even cooler Hawaiian shirt. Two sets from each act.

NOV. 25, BLACK SHEEP BOOKS, Vancouver, 2742 W.4th Ave., 732-5087, FREE
An intimate solo reading with guitar & bongos in a very cool bookstore. There will be coffee.

NOV. 26, JAVA CAFE, Victoria, 537 Johnson St., 381-2326, $2
We're still figuring out the ferry schedules, so please call first to make sure this is on.

DEC. 11, RAILWAY CLUB, Vancouver, 579 Dunsmuir, 681-1621, COVER
As above, this is with THE VAN PELT TRIO (Janis, Gord, & Bernie).

THE BEAT'S IN THE MAIL, MAN!

Here is the Official Ralph Mail Order Catalog. Order lots. All prices include postage.

THE MORNINGSIDE TAPE; complete Gzowski interview on cassette, $3
THE DEMO-LISTEN TAPE, the interview that started it all. One poem, lots of talking! $3
THE MORNINGSIDE POEMS, all 7 poems in a special zine just like this one, $1
THE ZERO AVENUE TV SHOW, a VHS of my appearance, $6
BACK ISSUES OF RALPH, the original printings are all SOLD OUT! (Snooze you looze) B/W laser copies are available instead for every issue, $1 ea.
THE DIODES, Survivors, a 1982 vinyl lp I actually produced & mixed of punk pop, $10

HAPPY BIRTHDAY TO ME! This is the 3rd anniversary issue (I debuted Nov., 1992)

THANKS! to Pam McGaha and Judith Beeman for helping me print last issue!
NEXT MONTH: My Baby Makes Great Sculptures, But I Make A Lousy Subject

RALPH is published monthly. Written & silk screened one page at a time on 1950s Gestetner duplicating machines by RALPH ALFONSO. Correspondence to: RALPH, Box 505 - 1288 Broughton St., Vancouver, BC, CANADA, V6G 2B5. My e.mail address is: ralpha6982@aol.com. My design skills are for hire. TEL: 604-654-2929 or FAX: 604-654-1993 (be cool, both are work numbers). **THIS IS A LIMITED EDITION PRINTING OF:** 3100 (oh my back!). ©1994 by Ralph Alfonso. Distributed by hand or by mail to cool people and places all over. I'll mail you a copy every month if you send me 12 Canadian stamps or $$$ equivalent ($5 in the USA & 12 x IRCs outside North America).

FREE   No. 23, Dec. 1994

RALPH
COFFEE, JAZZ, & POETRY

TI AMO PER CHE

io ti amo
per che
non so niente
di te
ma questa voce
in me
mi parle di te

I love you
I don't know why
I don't know anything
about you
But there's a voice
inside me
Always talking
about you

I WOULD REALLY LIKE TO KISS YOU BUT I CAN'T SEE WITHOUT MY GLASSES

Baby
Funny bumping into you
We're two round corners
in a square world
I guess we're two left feet
trying to find their way
I'm glad I tripped
I'm glad you fell
I never realized
picking up the pieces
was so much fun
I would really like
to kiss you
but
I can't see without my glasses

I LOVED YOU WELL, NEVER MIND

The bells are ringing
It's Christmas time
I got your card
And you got mine
I loved you
Well, never mind
It was just
A waste of time

I LOVE CHRISTMAS I LOVE YOU

I love Christmas
I love you
We can watch the big stars
All night through

No matter how cold
The wind may blow
I love
Walking in the snow

There is heaven in all of this
When we hold still for a kiss

IF THERE IS ONLY ONE SMILE IN YOUR LIFE, LET SOMEONE SEE IT JUST ONE NIGHT

This one night
I pray
For God's will
be done this day

Let every tear be still
Let every heart be filled
If there is only one smile
In your life
Let someone see it
Just one night

DON'T GET TOO CLOSE YOUR HAIR MIGHT POKE MY EYES OUT

Baby, you look good
Mmm, white lipstick
Tastes like wood
Everything you wear is
Shiny and Black
When you're in heels, honey
You never look back
In this great masquerade
I am a gentleman of leather
(My heart stays cold
In every kind of weather)
We're the bookends to
An empty book
I got the ending
But you got The Look

(WALKIN' THRU THE) SLEEPY CITY

The blue neon signs
shed a pale light on the
snow-covered streets
that you and I are walking through
watching the little mists of
cold air float up every time
we speak

And in this wonderful place
At the top of the world
on this empty corner
we stop under a street lamp
and we hold each other tight
we kiss
But it's so cold -
our lips stick together.

MY PAINTING IS TAKING A LONG TIME TO DRY

Well, I'm still waiting
for the paint to dry
on my beautiful painting
that I can't pick up
because I might smudge it
It's been five days now,
when you walk in
and catch me
using your hair dryer on it
Maybe I should have paid
more attention
in class,
There's probably some trick to this
bet
No wonder artists are so miserable

IT'S A DRAG THAT YOU HATE ME, 'CAUSE YOU'RE MY ONLY FRIEND

It's a drag that you hate me
'Cause you're my only friend
I hope you'll still call
Even if you yell at me
It's better than talking to myself
You know that's not healthy

BEAT FOR THE HOLIDAYS

the fireplace
warm
and you and I
together

maybe there's snow
or maybe not

flames on the candles
melting wax

nighttime - stars are out
and
scratchy records
(real music will never wear out)

drink hot coffee
from a bottomless cup

it's nothing
but it's everything...
if it makes you smile

BLEAT FOR THE HOLIDAYS!

I'll be pouring a little Baileys in my coffee this Xmas here in the cramped confines of The Beat Nook inside Box 505 to wish you the best over the Holidays, and then I'll pour just a little itsy bitsy more in there (oh heck, maybe just a TAD more) & see what ol' Santa put in the stocking (fishnet?) this year (GOSH! Baileys!). Oh, Oh, I'm about to visit the Coney Island of my mind (man), so, see you next year (Aw c'mon, Santa, just one more for the road here...) and stay cooool, baby!

IF I HAD A RADIO SHOW

The most unlikeliest of Christmas songs would be "September Girls" by Big Star, a litany of angst written by Alex Chilton (& yes! covered by The Bangles). Why? Numerous references to 'December Boys' & the group's name itself, BIG STAR (get it?). Those familiar with it will spot my loving homage throughout this issue. Next up is the coolest Rolling Stones song most people have never heard, "(Walkin Thru The) Sleepy City" from an lp called METAMORPHOSIS (abkco) that was a collection of Stones out-takes & easily available used for cheap. Recorded in '64, The Stones, via producer Andrew Loog Oldham, pay homage to Phil Spector and his A CHRISTMAS GIFT FOR YOU lp.

DECEMBER BOYS GOT IT BAD

December has always been magical for me; this is when I fall in love most easily (sappy poems alert!). I am especially wary this year as all my grand romances seem to end up as scripts for melancholic foreign films starring Jean-Louis Trintignant (does that guy ever smile, you think?). Hopefully, by writing about it, I can jinx it and make it to Jan. 5 (my birthday) unscathed & then Capricorn reason can kick in to keep me steady til next year. Wish me luck!

COVER ILLUSTRATION

Another great cover by Miss Molly Kiely, originally from Kitchener, Ontario (home of Dave Sim), but now living in San Francisco. The second issue of her adults-only DIARY OF A DOMINATRIX comic is published soon by Fantagraphics Books. Molly is also a freelance illustrator & any correspondence of that nature can be sent to her c/o this address.

POETRY. MORE THAN JUST YOUR LAST ENTERTAINMENT CHOICE!

My adventures as a performer continue with 2 gigs this month plus a videotaped performance on SOUNDPROOF, a local cable show. I am accompanied by Tom Harrison (bongos/cool vocals), Michael Rummen (guitar) & Ron Stelting (exotic percussion) in what can best be described as 60s garage meets 50s Verve jazz with The Kinks in there, too. Basically, this sheet come to life.

DEC. 11, RAILWAY CLUB, Vancouver, 579 Dunsmuir, 681-1621, COVER This is with THE VAN PELT TRIO (Janis, Gord, & Bernie). Two sets from each group. Early show.

DEC. 28, RAILWAY CLUB, We are opening for my friend Veda Hille & this will be my special Christmas Losers & Loners show with lots of XMAS poetry. EARLY SHOW. One set only!

RALPH AT RETAIL

In Vancouver, visit BLACK SHEEP BOOKS, 2742 W.4th Ave., 732-5087, for RALPH posters & tapes or send me a stamp for a catalog. All monies go towards my costs (I just paid $1000 for a massive shipment of ink) plus postage to mail to bookstores everywhere. I lose money every month, so any contributions would be cool ($10 or more gets you a free Donovan CD & a year's subscription!)

RALPH RECOMMENDS

CHARLES BROWN, *Cool Christmas Blues* (Bullseye/Rounder). Snuggly mellow XMAS blues for two. Includes a reprise of his 50s hits, "Merry Christmas Baby," & "Please Come Home For Christmas", both covered by Chuck Berry, who owes more than some of his vocal inflections to Mr. Brown. BONUS! Check out the cool beret on the cover photo. Very Chuck!

THE RHINOS, *Fishing In The Fountain Of Youth* (Kinetic). I rarely stop my car to listen to a song on the radio, but I did just that for "A Fantastic Place To Be", a song that seems to capture all the optimism & naivete I espouse so much. AWESOME!

B-TRIBE, *Fiesta Fatale* (Atlantic). I can't get "You Won't See Me Cry" out of my head. Gypsy Kings with an ambient dance beat ala Deep Forest and a Vangelis sample, too!

OUT OF THIS WORLD, PLAY BALL!, IN THE WINK OF AN EYE, $4.95 each, postage included. Patrick Jenkins, 125 Roxborough St. W., Toronto, Ontario, M5R 1T9 (416-964-7571/fax: 416-964-2990). Awesome little flipbooks that turn into cute animated vignettes. I really like OUT OF THIS WORLD in which a hapless little alien in his saucer ends up on a girl's nose! Great for kids & guaranteed to have anyone who sees one wanting to draw a little flipbook of their own!

CHET BAKER, *Grey December* (Capitol). A re-issue of two 50s recording sessions that have never been on a complete lp before. Classic Chet at his most melancholy. Also around is the CHET BAKER, *Pacific Jazz Years Box Set*, the mother-lode! Chet was one prolific guy & Capitol is slowly re-issuing his classic Pacific Jazz/World Pacific catalogue (now if they would only do the same with Bud Shank!).

TONGUE TIED, $5, Tom Snyders, 201-1067 Granville St., Vancouver, BC, V6Z 1L4. If you've never seen an honest to goodness literary mag, this is a good one to start with. They also accept contributions (art/poetry/photos, etc), but buy a copy first.

THE SPITS (Box 67657, 567 Dundas St. W., Toronto, Ontario, M5T 3B8). $15, includes postage. The Leslie Spit Treoo (I actually designed their 1st CD) trim their name & a member & go the indie route for a sound more like their first album. If you poured a lot of coffee down the throat of Mazzy Star's singer & gave her guitarist a boot in the butt, it would sound like this.

RALPH is published monthly. Written & silk screened one page at a time on 1950s Gestetner duplicating machines by RALPH ALFONSO. Correspondence to: RALPH, Box 505 - 1288 Broughton St., Vancouver, BC, CANADA, V6G 2B5. My e.mail address is: ralpha6982@aol.com. My design skills are for hire. TEL: 604-654-2929 or FAX: 604-654-1993 (be cool, both are work numbers). **THIS IS A LIMITED EDITION PRINTING OF:** 3000 . ©1994 by Ralph Alfonso. Distributed by hand or by mail to cool people and places all over. I'll mail you a copy every month if you send me 12 Canadian stamps or $6 ($5 in the USA & 12 x IRCs outside North America). **If you would like to volunteer & help me print, please call.**

FREE No. 24, Jan. 1995

RALPH
COFFEE, JAZZ, & POETRY

YOU CAN PULL THE STRINGS BUT
I'LL ALWAYS BE A SOUR NOTE

MY WEDDING, DEC. 18, 1985

So, after waiting around at the altar for a while, I figured you weren't going to show, so I paid the preacher a hundred bucks and went into the little hall next door.

I sat down in front of the wedding cake and cut myself a big piece.

I was the only person there, because I'd told everybody else to go home after the first hour of waiting and looking awkward.

Well, since I'd already paid for everything, I figured I should get my money's worth.

Surprisingly enough, the fifth bottle of wine went down pretty easy.

I'd picked through most of the food trays and there seemed to be half a cake left. The little toy plastic bride was floating in a pitcher of water and the little groom was in my front jacket pocket.

I must have fallen asleep, because all of a sudden my dad was sitting across from me. He was pouring himself a drink, and getting ready to dig into a big plate of anti-pasto.

"Hey, Pops!"

"Hey, so how's sleeping beauty? This is good stuff here, so don't eat it all. I told your mom we'd bring some back."

"Hey, I'm really sorry, Dad..."

"Ehhh....Love...everything's different t now...."

My dad shrugged and topped up my glass.

"Hey Pop, remember that song you used to sing at home all the time and we had to yell at you to shut up?"

Well, we must have been a hell of a sight when the waiter came in to wrap up the food for us.

There I was, me and my dad, clinking glasses and singing a really loud horrible version of "VOLARE" over and over.

"VO-LA-RE...WOAH, OH, OH....CAN-TA-RE....
OH, OH, OH....NEL BLU DI PINTO DI BLUE....."

Boy oh boy, was my mom gonna give me a big smack on the head when I got home.

*With sincerest apologies to Domenico Modugno, the writer of "Volare" & the lesser known, but equally appropriate "Ciao, Ciao, Bambina"

FELICITY, ONLY

The Eiffel Tower
may be tall
and I'm sure
sometimes
even lonely
But
high above
these cobbled streets
where the wind blows
your perfume around me
it's here we kiss
my love is this
for you
Felicity, only

*A confection inspired after seeing a vintage clip of the great comedian Fernandel on the French TV-show, "Les Enfants de la Tele", singing his Music Hall classic, "Felicie, Aussi"

10 MATTHEW STREET

My ears are ringing
And the music's loud
We're gonna dance all night
And never sit down
Twist, Hully Gully,
and The Limbo, too
It's gonna be all right
Now that I found you

*10 Matthew Street was the address of The Cavern Club, Liverpool. As long as you got a dime, that jukebox will never stop

COOKIES

Cookies are wonderful
They're light
and they're strong
Just one little bite
and then
they are gone

THIS IS MY CORNER OF THE WORLD

This is my corner of the world
This is where I make my stand
There's room for two
If you need a hand

It's a place where not everything works
But it's loved just the same
And maybe not everything's new
But some things get better with age

This is my little plot of land
My little net when the rest of
The world falls down
And it doesn't matter if
You forget that I'm even around
Quite frankly, sometimes
I'd rather not be found

*Driving over Granville Bridge in Vancouver early one morning watching the sun rise over the city, I found myself listening to Blossom Dearie singing a French version of "It Might As Well Be Spring" & the phrase "loin d'ici" (far from here) just stuck in my head. The song is about running away from the sadness of day to day & here I was already at that destination thinking about where I ran way from, & maybe if I made an effort to look into my own heart, I'd find that I already had what I was looking for.

FAR FROM HERE

Somewhere there are memories I hold dear
Some happy dreams that may bring a tear
But all of that is somewhere
Far from here

Somewhere there's a smile so full of cheer
A warm glow that is always near
But all of that is somewhere
Far from here

Somewhere there's a heart inside here
And faith in these clouds to disappear
But all of that is somewhere
Far from here

SAMBA FOR TWO

Baby, we can twist all night
You look great in this moonlight
And each night when
I sit down and pray
I thank God you're with me
Every day

We can mambo in Ipanema
Cha Cha Cha in old Brasil
Baby, you and me
We can hold hands
Down by the sea

Just one kiss
Is all that I ask for
Because you know that
Here and there
And everywhere
I love you

In this wonderful world
There is always a samba for two

*I wrote this for my friends The Van Pelt Trio who asked me to read it on stage during what would normally be the sax solo in "The Girl From Ipanema", and if you read it out loud to the album version, it should last the duration of the solo. Try it.

DAVE SMELTZER
In Memoriam

This issue is dedicated to my friend Dave Smeltzer, owner of The Bop Shop on Queen St. in Toronto, who passed away in his sleep the week before Christmas. Dave was one of the nicest & most knowledgeable record collectors I have ever known. A lot of the records and music books I own I probably bought from Dave. From his days at Records On Wheels in 1976 when we first met, to his work at The Record Peddler/Fringe, to finally his own shop, Dave was always there to support the Toronto indie scene. Our friendship over the years was always about music and having his own shop was a source of great happiness for him. Dave left this world in his apartment at the store, surrounded by the music he loved, on the street that had provided most of it. Toronto is less interesting without him.
Play it loud, wherever you are, buddy.

FOLLOW YOUR HEART, THE BRAIN WILL CATCH UP
As I enter my fourth year of publishing, I am happy in the knowledge that while I may not be able to follow the script, at least I've got the plot.

COVER ILLUSTRATION
Michael Lennea is a Vancouver illustrator with a fine hand for turn of the century illustration. His line drawings of historical buildings are especially cool. He is available for freelance work at 604-737-0866 or 604-271-6175.

GOATEE ON CD --- OH NO! RALPH IN THE STUDIO!
My Vancouver subscribers will have already gotten their invites to join me for a live recording session, Jan. 21, at Slack Studios where we'll try to bring old fashioned vibes to a state-of-the-art 24-Track ADAT studio. When the engineers asked me for an idea of what I'm after, I showed them the pictures on the back of my old Ramsey Lewis lps where everybody's having a cool time. Look for a CD possibly by March or April (yes, the book is next).

FEB 3, CBC FM RADIO, 11PM, NIGHT LINES WITH DAVID WISDOM, I am hosting an "Hour Of Power", playing very cool sounds from my record collection plus reading a poem or two!

FEB 5, GRUNT GALLERY, Vancouver
We are the opening act for author Lynn Crosbie. EARLY SHOW.

FEB 14, GLASS SLIPPER, Vancouver, 2714 Prince Edward, 877-0066
We will represent the positive at this VALENTINE'S DAY event. Other poets, TBA, will reveal me for the idealistic chump dreamer I really am. Beautiful venue. Nice stage.

GOATEE TO GO! MAIL ORDER STUFF
Contributions of $10 or more gets you a year's subscription plus a free Donovan Tribute CD (Various Artists) on Nettwerk that I designed. Send a stamp for a catalog of tapes, posters, back issues, etc.

RALPH RECOMMENDS

THE COLORIFICS, *Girlie Door*, $7, #301-309 Cordova, West Vancouver, BC, Canada, V6B 1E5. A very cool cassette of mellow retro jazzy sounds. Chanteuse Lindsay Davis is a cross between Astrud Gilberto & Françoise Hardy. Highly recommended!!

SAVOY JAZZ RE-ISSUE SERIES, Denon Records bought the rights to this pioneering jazz, R&B, & gospel label & is re-issuing lots of stuff on CD. Of what I've heard, I like these cause they are sweet & mellow: THE PERRY ROBINSON 4, *Funk Dumpling*; CHUCK WAYNE, BREW MOORE, ZOOT SIMS, *Tasty Pudding*; CANNONBALL ADDERLEY, *Discoveries*.

BOB BERG, *Virtual Reality* (Denon). Cool late-night sax. Will Lee on bass.

THE JAZZ SCENE, (Various Artists, Verve); The best $30 I've spent all year! A beautiful 2CD set packaged like an old 78rpm album. Incredible!! Strayhorn, Young, Hawkins, Ellington, Parker, Buddy Rich, Powell, etc. etc. Look for the black & yellow cover. A re-issue of the rarest Verve album.

RAGING HORMONES, *Bare As You Dare*, $10, 4936 Yonge St., #145, North York, Ontario, M2N 6S3. This came with a note from singer Arch Rockefeller thanking me for my help 12 years ago (this brought a Frank Capra tear to my eye!) when I tried to get him signed to Stiff Records. If you think Jona Lewie meets David Wilcox is of interest (see "BIG BABY"), check it out. Very tacky artwork!

SCHLOCK, *The Journal of Low-Brow Cinema & Culture*, $1, John Chilson, 3841 Fourth Ave., #192, San Diego, CA, USA, 92103. Amazing tabloid newspaper with in-depth reviews of the latest bad-videos, weird zines & feature articles on The Monkees HEAD movie, Sue Lyon (LOLITA), & my fave, a run-down of all cool movies that feature people on Vespas!!! John used to be in The Hoods.

DEVLIN THOMPSON, 475 Metgs St., #3, Athens, GA, USA, 30601. Devlin publishes all sorts of neato stuff. Send him $5 & he'll send you an envelope full of mini-comics, cool stickers & things.

WORLD LETTER, $5, c/o Jon Cone, 2726 E. Court St., Iowa City, IA, USA, 52245.
A more traditional literary review if you're ready to graduate from RALPH to the real thing.

SISTER LOVERS, Box 78069, 2606 Commercial Drive, Vancouver, BC, V5N 5W1. If I could be in a pure pop band, I would choose SISTER LOVERS. Check their 45, "PAULA STOP PRETENDING" (an ode to the late Paula Pierce of The Pandoras) or the cheesy home video I did the cover for. Ask for a catalog & say I sent you (they're the only people who think I'm cool cause I worked with BRIGHTON ROCK).

RALPH is published monthly. Written & silk screened one page at a time on 1950s Gestetner duplicating machines by RALPH ALFONSO. Correspondence to: RALPH, Box 505 - 1288 Broughton St., Vancouver, BC, CANADA, V6G 2B5. My e.mail address is: ralpha6982@aol.com. My design skills are for hire. TEL: 604-654-2929 or FAX: 604-654-1993 (be cool, both are work numbers). **THIS IS A LIMITED EDITION PRINTING OF:** 3000 . ©1995 by Ralph Alfonso. Distributed by hand or by mail to cool people and places all over. I'll mail you a copy every month if you send me 12 Canadian stamps or $6 ($5 in the USA & 12 IRCs outside North America). CLICK MY NAME AT THIS WEB PAGE! URL: http://www.wimsey.com/nettwerk/

FREE   No. 25, Feb. 1995

RALPH
COFFEE, JAZZ, & POETRY

FEBRUARY'S A GOOD MONTH TO BE BAD

GOODBYE WINNIPEG, FEB. 1988

Our last night in Winnipeg
Oh what a nightmare
It's bad enough
It's so cold
It just makes me miserable
And then your mom
Gave me a nice speech
She really liked me
But
Honestly
You and I were not going to work out
If I was smart
I would know what to do
Gee, thanks a lot
I didn't really get mad
I just got in the car
And drove down the big wide roads
Past the college
Up Portage St., till I turned
into Polo Park Mall
And just sat in my black Ford Granada
Listening to the crappy music
From the crappy radio station I
was parked in front of
Drinking a crappy coffee
(That was the one good thing
about Winnipeg
They'll never make a decent
Fancy pants coffee here)
I heard a tapping on the window
You knew I was going to end up here
So you had a cab follow me
And now we were
Sitting in the front seat
It was quiet for a minute
Except for the crappy 70s rock song on the radio
And we sort of looked at each other
I saw the 7-Eleven bag on your lap
You pulled out a Diet-Coke for yourself
You waited a second
And then out came
A big box of ripple chips
I can't remember who
Started laughing first

THERE IS STILL A SUN WHEN IT RAINS

There is still a sun
When it rains
That's why I'm deaf
When you complain
Aches and pains
Are
Your domain
Sun and sand
Still
My terrain

OH NO, I CAN'T FIND THE KEYS TO MY HEART!

I'm hurrying as fast
As I can
I can't find all the keys
For all the locks
Strapped around
This heart
The secret codes
And combinations
The cobwebs and dust
Everything stuck
With the rust
And when the sunlight
Reaches in
Ah, what a sigh!
You and I

VALENTINE IN HEAVEN

When I saw you
Standing at the gates
of Heaven
I fell right through
these clouds
If there's ever
anything I can do
I would even gather up
each morning's dew
Just for this chance
to be with you

MY SHIP IS COMING IN BUT I GOT DRUNK AND FELL OFF

My ship is coming in
But I got drunk
And fell off
I hope someone is
Still around
To throw me
A raft
I can't swim
They'd better hurry
I think I see
A fin

MY SCRAPBOOK OF HAPPINESS IS MISSING A FEW PAGES, I GUESS

My scrapbook of happiness
Is missing a few pages, I guess
I used to have more
Now I settle for less

DON'T WORRY IT'LL SOON BE DECEMBER AGAIN

Don't worry
It'll soon be December again
We'll be together
When snowflakes fall again
And quiet nights
Watching stars twinkle again
And whisper things
Over coffee again
Don't worry
This heart will always burn the flame
To guide our lips when
They touch again

THAT'S THE DRAG ABOUT LOVE I ALWAYS FAIL THE TEST

I miss the way
You ignored me
Every day
I miss the look
That told me
Go away
I miss the little things
You never said
Or did
I miss my wallet
You always liked it best
That's the drag about love
I always fail the test

SUDBURY DAYS

In the moment's passion
We knew
Here in God's desolate country
Two lonely hearts
Can pause
From disparate journeys

I JUST CAN'T BELIEVE THE THINGS I DON'T SAY

I just can't believe
The things I don't say
The words that can't
Quite make it up
My throat and out my lips
(That would dearly love to
meet yours, by the way)
The brain and I
We just can't believe this heart
Getting tired
After a few false starts
Just suck in some fresh air
And go for it
We say

COVER ILLUSTRATION

Hmm, it appears my first date in almost 3 years isn't going so well. Hopefully, I'll escape in time for next issue. Mr. Tom Bagley delivers another exceptional cover masterpiece! Tom, in his other guise as Jackson Phibes, is the lead/singer guitarist of Calgary's horror-boogie rockers THE FORBIDDEN DIMENSION. For a catalog of stuff, write c/o Box 3269, Bankview RPO, Calgary, AB, Canada, T2T 5X6. Obscure trivia: The cover is actually a tribute to the "Phoebe Zeitgeist" comic-strip that used to appear in EVERGREEN magazine in the mid-60s. (Hmm. Do you think we're a little too obsessed with 60s trash Americana?)

RALPH READS YOUR MAIL

More back page. Less footnotes. More footnotes. Less poems. More Gothic. More jazz. Where's the book. Where's the CD. The big fish in Kenora is called "Huskie The Muskie". They don't have bumper boats in Salmon Arm anymore. Nice fonts. You've really got to stop living in this nostalgia about your ex-girlfriends, let's face it, you were a doormat (an actual quote from an ex-girlfriend). How can it be a limited edition if you print 3000. How do you make money. Do you write all this yourself. Are you a beatnik. Is all this stuff true.

THANKS FOR YOUR CONCERN

But MY WEDDING last month, altho based on bits and pieces of mine & other people's stories & bringing them to an inevitable conclusion, is otherwise fiction. The material in RALPH is not meant to be autobiographical.

GET YER GOATEES OUT

FEB 11, VOGUE THEATRE, Vancouver, The NETTWERK 10th Anniversary Concert. We are on for 10 minutes starting at 8:30pm. Sold Out, so come early if you have a ticket.

FEB 14, GLASS SLIPPER, Vancouver, 2714 Prince Edward, 877-0066 How cool is this?! Veda Hille & I will do a short set together in addition to dueting on a surprise 50s standard. Also joining us for the RALPH segment will be our new cool piano addition, Tracey Marks (looking very Jazzbo). Beautiful venue. Nice stage.

CAN IT BE? THE RALPH CD

The RALPH CD session went great & we even cut a whole set of very Deep Lounge™ Italo-flavoured all-original saloon-style songs. If you dig Dino - I could be the sparkle in your vino (grooan!). It's a very ambitious, yet casual, collection of spoken word, jazz, garage rock, latin & lounge. It is all yours for $15 (including postage). Order now so I can pay for the manufacturing of it. Available in April. ALSO NOTE: Contributions of $10 or more (for the Ralph cause) gets you a year's subscription (for you or a friend) plus a free Donovan Tribute CD (Var Artists) on Nettwerk that I designed. Send a stamp for a catalog of tapes, posters, back issues, etc.

RALPH RECOMMENDS

SECOND GUESSING, *The Beautiful Ugly*, $7, Kenn Sakurai, 3573 West 16th Ave, Basement Suite, Vancouver, BC, V6R 3C2. This group only exists to produce cool cassette albums of 80s synth & textured pop ala Duran, Flock Of Seagulls, Spoons, Rational Youth et al., very cool.

THE ONE, *Cultured Palate* (Dwarf Records). Mini-CD return of Peter Perrett (ex-Only Ones singer/creative force). It sounds as dreamy as you thought it would. Check import shops.

YOU RIDE A HORSE RATHER LESS WELL THAN ANOTHER HORSE WOULD, $1, Box 44090 - 6518 E. Hastings St., Burnaby, BC, V5B 4Y2. Totally keen zine with lots of movie, zine & music reviews in that neat cut & paste DIY style that's a cut above the rest.

MORE STUFF BY SOME DUMB GIRL, $1, Sharon, 8 Louis Ave., St. Catharines, ON, L2M 2N5. A really charming little booklet of short poems & thoughts kind of like a female version of RALPH.

GRAFFITO, $1, Friday Circle, Dept. of English, U of Ottawa, K1N 6N5. Neat tabloid poetry sheet that accepts contributions (poems must not be longer than 30 lines).

PASADENA AFTER HOURS, $1, David Young, 4200 Pasadena Place NE, #2, Seattle, WA, USA, 98105-6064. 20page mini-comic in a Life In Hell vein. Cool humour.

SOMETHING HAS HIT ME, £1.50, Mark Raison, 44 Lawrence Dr., Ickenham, Middlesex, UB10 8RW, England. Awesome zine devoted to cool 60s British Beat.

THANKS TO KENN SAKURAI & JURGEN SCHAUB FOR HELPING ME PRINT LAST ISSUE

RALPH is published monthly. Written & silk screened one page at a time on 1950s Gestetner duplicating machines by RALPH ALFONSO. Correspondence to: RALPH, Box 505 - 1288 Broughton St., Vancouver, BC, CANADA, V6G 2B5. My e.mail address is: ralpha6982@aol.com. My design skills are for hire. TEL: 604-654-2929 or FAX: 604-654-1993 (be cool, both are work numbers). **THIS IS A LIMITED EDITION PRINTING OF:** 3000 (lots!). ©1995 by Ralph Alfonso. Distributed by hand or by mail to cool people and places all over. I'll mail you a copy every month if you send me 12 Canadian stamps or $6 ($5 in the USA & 12 x IRCs outside North America). FIND ME AT THIS WEB PAGE! URL: http://www.wimsey.com/nettwerk

COFFEE, JAZZ, & POETRY

$1.00

RALPH

THE MORNINGSIDE POEMS

SPECIAL EDITION • HORS SERIE

THIS DOMINION

Drunk up on the hill in St. John's,
Newfoundland, watching the waves hit the
rocks below, stopping on the highway
because there's a giant moose in the road,
crawling in and out of every bar on that
street, you know the one I mean, baby,
this proud dominion, on the boat to
Charlottetown, that Sunday flea market,
you knew I wasn't from there, was I,
and all these Nova Scotia backroads,
quiet hamlets God has blessed with Celtic
fervour, these cobblestone streets of
Amherst, falling asleep on this ferry from
St. John, New Brunswick, to God knows
where, Quebec City, we kissed in the
middle of snow and fortresses, and
fireworks in Montreal, Sunday dinners in
Elora, Fergus flea market, looking for old
records in Hamilton, and Toronto...
I miss you baby, but you broke my heart.
And so Sudbury, Thunder Bay, Kenora
(nice fish), Winnipeg, we walked along the
sand no one knows about, I'm sorry
you tried to show me your world when
I was still trying to figure out mine. But, we
all have a place in this great dominion, to
live and let its beauty heal all wounds.

PERFORMANCE

You probably didn't see me
I was sitting in the back.
Everything you did on stage
Made absolutely no sense to me.
Why someone as beautiful as you
Could be involved with such
Caterwauling, I'll never know
You must be a lonely breed,
The Performance Artist.
I felt ill at ease
Knowing I was the only one there
Without a body odour
I was hoping no one would notice.
Maybe it's just envy
From all of us
Filling our endless notebooks,
Maintaining an English language
Hardly anyone reads,
Thanks to your de-construction
Of what's good, what's bad.
But more importantly...
You look pretty pale,
You must not be eating well.

THE GOATEE CLUB

I don't know how I got into this one
Sitting around, drinking beer
with a bunch of weird guys
from The Goatee Club
I thought my life was bad
But not until I met these characters
They're like
A walking sponge of misery
And everybody's kind of checking
each other out
Gotta be careful what you say
It could end up as somebody else's poem

a long kiss in the rain

Wet sidewalks; mirrors for neon lights,
empty restaurants, and rain-soaked
newspapers kicked out of the way.

We couldn't think of anything to say.
She stirred her coffee again. I lit a
cigarette. She picked at her cake.
I thought, well, what a mistake this
was.

At least she smiled when she realized
it, too, and held a forkful of crumbly-
something at my mouth. I said some-
thing funny. I liked to see her laugh.

Just a mild drizzle in the parking lot.
I open the car door for her, but before
she can get in, I hold her; right there -
for a long kiss in the rain.

IT'S A WONDERFUL WORLD
(if you know someone in it)

I guess
I'm a paid up member
of the lonely club
A connoisseur of
the cigarette stub

And
in life's parade
if I'm a clown
at least you're smiling
when I'm around

Yes
it's a wonderful world
if you know someone in it
it's a wonderful world
if you know your place

crawling around in the fountain

It's way past midnight
I have no idea what I had been drinking
but, man, was my brain on a
rocket to the moon
which, incidentally, is
practically the only light I've got
here right now
knee-deep and flailing around
in this fountain in the middle of Rome
looking for the pennies I threw
in here
years ago, with this girl
it turns out
I hardly knew
Man, I lost some really good wishes
that never had a chance
to come true
So I figure, hell, I'm here
If I can get those coins back
I can try again
next time I've got something in mind
for the future
But
now I'm completely dripping wet
and some woman is yelling at me
in crazy Italian from some window
up the street
And I'm thinking, oh no
not now
when I slip on the guck
and swing my hands out in front of me
so I don't hit bottom
and I grab a bunch of coins and
run splashing down
the little cobblestone streets
with two cops giving chase
But it doesn't matter
I found my little Canadian penny
And now I'm back at the start

RIFFIN'

Got a note, Blow a note
Wrote a note, Quote a note
Sent a note, Read a note
Saw a note, Drop a note
Change a note, Play a note
Flip a note, Float a note
And on this note...
please add your notes

Ralph   mike   Tom

1. THIS DOMINION
2. PERFORMANCE
3. THE GOATEE CLUB
4. A LONG KISS IN THE RAIN
5. IT'S A WONDERFUL WORLD
   (IF YOU KNOW SOMEONE IN IT)
6. CRAWLING AROUND IN THE FOUNTAIN
7. RIFFIN'

Ralph Alfonso read these poems, Oct. 3, 1994, on "MORNINGSIDE" with Peter Gzowski and broadcast on the CBC-AM national radio network.

With musical accompaniment by:
Michael Rummen, *guitar*
Tom Harrison, *cool vocals and bongos*

Written & silk screened one page at a time on 1950s Gestetner duplicating machines by RALPH ALFONSO. Correspondence to: RALPH, Box 505 - 1288 Broughton St., Vancouver, BC, CANADA, V6G 2B5. My e.mail address is: ralpha6982@aol.com. TEL: 604-654-2929 or FAX: 604-654-1993 (be cool, both are work numbers). ©1995 by Ralph Alfonso. My neat poetry zine, RALPH, is distributed by hand or by mail to cool people and places all over. I'll mail you a copy every month if you send me 12 Canadian stamps or $6. ($5 in the USA & 12 x IRCs outside North America).
THIS IS A LIMITED EDITION PRINTING OF: 300. Illustrations by the author.

RALPH

PREVIOUSLY UNPUBLISHED POETRY & ILLUSTRATIONS
PLUS SCRAPBOOK PHOTOS, POSTERS AND STUFF

WHAT I READ THIS MONTH by Ralph Alfonso

Ever wonder what People Are Reading? I do. **Ralph Alfonso**, way kool author of the wondrous freebie poetry explosion called *Ralph*, took the time to write and tell **subtext**.

Like everybody else I find that the older I get the less time I seem to have to put aside for serious reading, so these days I like to go through several sources at once; kind of like channel-hopping through paper.

During the last two months, I've enjoyed *Kicks!*, a great 50's/60's trash rock fanzine edited by the ultimate rock couple: Billy Miller & Miriam Linna (They're in a band together. They edit a fanzine together. They run a label together.). They once stayed at my place when I lived in Toronto and, oddly enough, I've never heard from them since. I got it at Track Records (who also carry *Cryptic Tymes*, a kind of local equivalent).

The subject of comic books can get me going for hours, but I'll be positive and say I like *Eightball, Magnus, Grendel, Mr. Monster, Madman, E.C. Reprints,* and *Spawn* (well, we're not all perfect).

Book-wise, I just got *Mostly Harmless* by Douglas Adams, *Heart of the World* by Nik Cohn (his Ball the Wall compilation proves why he was the ultimate 60's Mod-rock journalist), *Beyond Co-Dependency* by Melody Beatty (you'll be surprised), plus *The Art of Blue Note* and *California Cool* (two amazing books with page after page of 50's jazz LP covers).

A cool newspaper to get is the weekly *European*, a kind of Euro *USA Today* that covers what's happening over there with more meat than you find in the local papers (no comment). You have to keep a world perspective on things which, if you can read French, I would recommend picking up the Thursday edition of *Liberation* down at Manhattan Books (you can find it on the French newspaper rack on the 2nd floor). It's their weekly Arts round-up & a pretty cool poster item to casually have lying around.

Ralph is available by subscription @12 issues for 12 First Class stamps or monetary equivalent: $5.16.

DISCORDER, March 1993, 'Subtext' column by Judith Beeman

RALPH

#19, July 1994. I found this in a coffee shop, and Ralph must travel a lot because he covers San Francisco this time with a bit of Punk history, a Jennifer Joseph reading, a trip to North Beach and City Lights, and a poem that almost makes fun of poetry. There's also a list of Ralph's latest reads, and a feeling in this short publication comes from the heart and travels of a man who wants to know what life is all about. Price: $1. P.O. Box 505-1288 Broughton St., Vancouver, BC V6G 2B5, Canada (4 pages/O)

FACTSHEET FIVE #54

January, 1995

ARTISTS & REPERTOIRE

Nettwerk Records BBQ, 1994
Ralph, Mike and Tom
Note the candles.

Goatee Nation rallies around *Ralph*

Ralph is a fanzine. Ralph is a beatnik quartet. Ralph is Ralph Alphonso, former punk impresario, Attic Records publicist and major label marketing guy turned west coast computer design guru for Nettwerk Productions, Plum Records and indie acts galore. Ralph's new-found celebrity status is based on his self-penned, self-produced, self-titled poetry monthly, which he lovingly cranks out by hand on an antique Gestetner copier. Among his 3,000 readers are some CBC Radio types who asked him to recite a few choice poems — The Goatee Club and *It's A Wonderful World (If You Know Someone In It)*, though they overlooked *I Love You Baby But You Gotta Stop Wearing Those Ugly Shoes* — on a recent Morningside. Seeking to enliven his guest shot with Peter Gzowski, Alphonso enlisted music critic/bongo player Tom Harrison and guitarist Michael Rummen to play sympathetic jazz licks. The vibes were so profoundly cool that the trio volunteered to perform at the annual Nettwerk BBQ in late September. Half-way through the set up jumped former Odds drummer Paul Brennan to solidify the beat. Laughs Ralph: "He said afterwards he felt compelled to come up. It's a great band, now we've just got to expand our repertoire beyond 15 minutes."

The newly-minted quartet moves on to a 'Hey! How 'Bout Those 50s?' show at Vancouver's Malcolm Lowry Room on Nov. 24. With the added bonus of the Van Pelt Trio, a jazz ensemble led by Gord Badanic of Zulu Records, it's billed as "a very cozy evening of cool jazz, cigarettes, martinis, sharp suits, beatniks, berets, goatees and poetry."

Superior java is guaranteed.

THE RECORD
Nov. 7, 1994. Story by Jeff Bateman.

HEY! HOW 'BOUT THOSE 50S?

JULIE LONDON MEETS JACK KEROUAC FOR DRINKS AT A TAWDRY BAR IN NORTH BURNABY FOR A VERY COZY EVENING OF COOL JAZZ, CIGARETTES, MARTINIS, SHARP SUITS, BEATNIKS, BERETS, GOATEES, AND POETRY

A VERY COOL EVENING WITH

the Van Pelt Trio

one neat girl in a chiffon gown,
two cool guys in sharp suits,
lots & lots of jazz standards

RALPH

Ralph Alfonso & three of his beatnik pals with bongos, guitar, goatees, coffee, jazz & poetry

4125 E. HASTINGS
FREE ADMISSION
685-0143

MALCOLM LOWRY ROOM. NOV. 24

The very first live club show. Each group did 2 sets.

*This was a very magical night. While waiting for the musicians to show up,
I did an impromptu solo reading, answered questions and took requests (sad poems? happy stuff?).*

TWIST AT ST. TROPEZ

A beautiful kiss.
A beautiful girl.
It must be love on the French Riviera.
A fast little Peaugot racing along the coast.
A warm day at the beginning of summer.

The two of them had just been in Cannes,
watching rich tourists spend money.
Now they sat at an outdoor cafe,
looking at the sailboats and yachts
laze around the Mediterranean.

Ice cream and black cappuccino.
They laughed.
He lit her cigarette.
She took off his sunglasses.
He shook his head.
She was a wild one.
He loved it.
Her white jeans,
black sweater, suede jacket.
He leaned over for a kiss.

Now the Peaugot sputtered
into a little parking lot.
It was night time in St. Tropez.
This was the club
where everyone came to dance.
Crowded.
Full of smoke.
You dance close.
You dance apart.
You borrow cigarettes.
Talk to friends.

And then it was later.
Full moon.
Long kiss.
The Peaugot roared
back onto the highway.

LE ROI DE RIEN

un royaume sans personnes
je suis le roi
de rien

j'attends les paroles
qui vient sur le vent

There's the sound
of the wind
nothing else
so it seems
this is my kingdom
of nothing
only stars
and moon beams

A BREED APART

It was a lovely affair
Everyone was there
Some broken hearts
Some brand new starts
And those of us
A breed apart

NEXT MORNING'S CIGARETTE IS HANGING ON HER ASHTRAY

Next morning's cigarette
is hanging on her ashtray
I'm holding on to her warmth
While the cat in the corner
wishes I'd just go away

I LOVE YOU BABY, BUT

Well, hey
How about that
I seem to have run out of money
Maybe we could sell
One of those fabulous
things I've bought you
So I can eat
next week

ME NOT RECOGNIZING MYSELF

I used to feel
like
I had been abandoned
but
it was just
me not recognizing myself

ANYTHING ELSE YOU CAN HAVE IT ALL

Everything you need
Is everything
I will try to be

Have faith
In case I stumble
Trust
In case I fall

As long as you have my heart
Anything else
You can have it all

JUST A MOMENT WITHOUT GRAVITY

Just a moment
without gravity
To study the shell I
have inherited
and what repairs
it hungers most for
That I can solder
from within

IF I COULD DEAL WITH THE WORLD THROUGH THE MAIL

If I could deal
with the world
through the mail
I'd be a lot happier

I MUST BE THE FELLOW THAT SOMEONE FORGOT

In life's parade
If I'm a clown
At least you're smiling
When I'm around

And all the good fortune
That everyone got
I must be fellow
that someone forgot

But for all these worries
I can't complain
I would gladly start over
All over again

EXTRA LITTLE KISSES

1. Your lips hold a smile
that I must kiss
for a long long while

2. Love is a funny thing
You never know
How much kisses
It will bring

3. It's the smile
That will always be
My master and
Saviour from disaster

4. A phone call to your heart
Is always answered

5. The smile of a child
Hair sometimes wild
This is the girl that
I love

IT WAS CRAZY WHEN WE MET

It was crazy when we met
We got sucked into the vacuum of
each other's malcontent
The initial euphoria of kindred spirit
was soon blown away by the realization of
what am I doing living with this misfit?
It's not right to be unhappy about finally
being happy
A wonderful future
turns into an awful present
I want to give back

Nettwerk Records
10th Anniversary
Concert,
Feb. 11, 1995
Vogue Theatre
Vancouver

left to right:
Michael Rummen
Tom Harrison
Ralph Alfonso
Ron Stelting

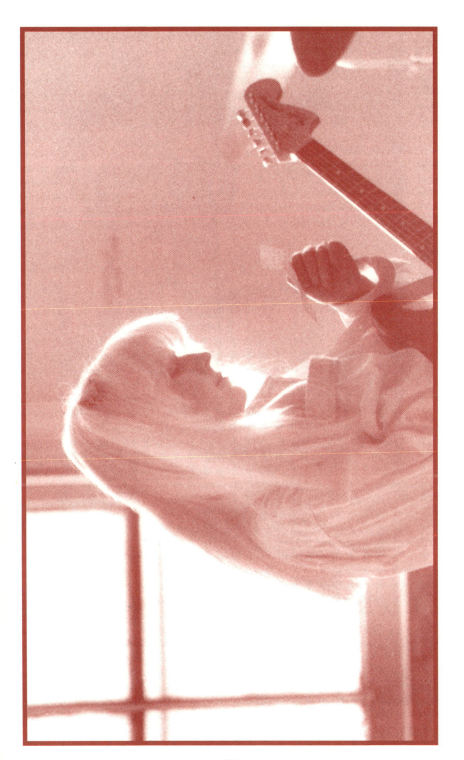

You and a guest are invited to attend
AN EVENING WITH RALPH
a live album recording session
Slack Studios, 1616 West 3rd Ave.
7:30 pm, Saturday, Jan. 21
Some beer & coffee will be provided but it's best to BYOB
LIMITED SEATING (40)
You must RSVP by calling Ralph at 654-2929

COOL
RALPH'S SO...

BY GORDON CAVENAILE

Ralph is cooler than you. He might even be cooler than me.

I mean, anybody that gets 27 minutes on Gzowski to recite quasi-beatnik poetry while two cats vamp behind him on bongos and guitar must be, you know, cool.

Not convinced?

Then dig this: Anybody who has a funky little fanzine named after himself must be full of poetry all about himself must be, like, yeah, you got it: cool.

Still a little skeptical? Well, let's try this face to face:

Anybody that mixes and matches long sensitive hippy hair with a jazzy little goatee, and sets off state of the art knee-freezing grunge jeans with artsy yellow glasses and green suede shoes must be, you know, like....

All right, Ralph can explain it in his own words.

"I'm in outer space."

Cool. But what's he doing there?

Among other things, working on Ralph—the fanzine, that is.

It's an eight by eleven piece of paper folded over to make four little pages, and it's printed on a '50s Gestetner hand printer. Subtitled "Coffee, Jazz, & Poetry," Ralph—the zine—appears once a month in places like Deluxe Junk or Cab-bages and Kinx, somewhere in the general vicinity of the Georgia Straight and the Pacific Cinemateque guide.

All 3,000 monthly copies of the zine are free, and—oddly, since the poet-publisher-printer stands goatee-deep in the jazz and beatnik traditions—they're all devoid of "intellectual stuff," as Ralph puts it.

"If you're a real beatnik elit-

Wayne Hoecherl photo

ist," Ralph said over coffee on Robson, "or if you're a real jazz snob, then the zine is not for you."

After you read lines like "Tell me/Who can resist/To hold your hand/To share a kiss", it's easy to see what Ralph means. This, after all, is a poet who found the future of his art form in the London Drug stationery section.

"Some of the best poetry today is on Hallmark cards," he said. "And some of my stuff is just as good."

Maybe, but how does jazz fit into all this?

"My attitude is the jazz attitude of post-war, up until the early sixties, which was very open. It was a period when people were creating the blueprints which people are now following."

That's a big clue. We have here one of those pop-acculturated late baby-boomers who took the time to trace the lineage of the '70s and '60s back through the '50s, and discovered that long before the Stones sneered and Kesey went psychedelic, Chuck Berry, Lawrence Ferlinghetti, and the jazzers were laying down the essence of cool.

There it is again: that WORD. It's hard to avoid around Ralph, so I lay the big question on him. What does cool mean, anyway?

"Martin Denny is cool. Mantovani is uncool."

Pretty esoteric, Ralph.

"Leonard Cohen is cool. Irving Layton is uncool."

A little easier on the head, but what's the difference?

"Maybe Layton's a better poet, who knows. Leonard was cool from the word go."

Of course.

Langara College, Vancouver, 1994

TV STAR

I was sitting outside,
trying to cool down
some coffee I'd ordered

She lit a cigarette and
started to cross the street
The sunglasses were a nice touch.

Of course
She had some sort of notoriety now
The TV show helped that.

I should have stopped her
Should have introduced myself
Hi there,
I was the guy you picked up
in a bar beside the TV studio

She walked right by...
I put some change down on the table
and got up to leave

I had to do it
I ran up behind her

"Excuse me,"
I said

Who is this guy
she must have thought

"...tell me...
do you still have that funny tattoo
on your left butt?"

LOVERS & LOSERS
VALENTINE'S DAY
TUES, FEB 14 • GLASS SLIPPER

2714 PRINCE EDWARD ST (12TH & KINGSWAY BEHIND THE BILTMORE HOTEL) • 877-0066

WHETHER YOU'RE FLAILING IN LOVE OR JUST LUCKY AT CARDS, YOU'LL ENJOY...

RALPH

COFFEE, JAZZ & POETRY with Ralph Alfonso, reading, singing & drinking coffee with his beatnik pals: Tom Harrison, bongos & vocals • Michael Rummen, guitar • Ron Stelting, percussion • Tracey Marks, piano

VEDA HILLE
solo poetry & song

JAY McLAUGHLIN
performing "KRÛSH"

THE DUCK TAPE PLATYPUS POETS COALITION
Rodney Decroo, Steve Duncan, Jim McAuliffe, Bernie Radelfinger

TONGUE OF THE SLIP #28
doors open at 8pm • show starts 9pm sharp
TICKETS AT THE DOOR
Souvenir Booklet Included With Admission
a panarky production

CREDITS

ILLUSTRATIONS:
TOM BAGLEY   p.55, 79, 99, 111, 120
PATRICK JENKINS   p.107
TOM KALICHAK   p.67
MICHAEL KALUTA   p.71
MOLLY KIELY   p.83, 91, 116-117, 122, 124
MICHAEL LENNEA   p.95
SCOTT SAAVEDRA   p.35
RALPH ALFONSO   p.3, 7, 10, 14-15, 26-27, 30, 59, 75, 103, 106, 108, 126

PHOTOGRAPHY:
TOM ROBE   p.31, 43
WAYNE HOECHERL   p.47, 114-115, 118 (top)
GARY LALONDE   p.39
CATHERINE MCLAREN   p.109
ALISON ROGERS   p.125
SVEN   p.118 (bottom)
RALPH ALFONSO   p.51, 63, 87, 119

ARCHIVAL PHOTOS:
CHET BAKER (William Claxton), ASTRUD GILBERTO (Jerry Schatzberg)
VINCE TAYLOR (unknown), FRANCOISE HARDY (J.M. Perier)

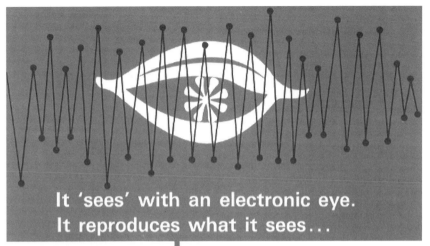

It 'sees' with an electronic eye.
It reproduces what it sees...

Fig.1 Ink is poured manually over the rollers.

Fig.2-3 Artwork is cut on a plastic stencil that wraps around a silkscreen. Turn the handle to print!

Fig.4 The actual Gestetner 120 that printed all the issues of RALPH reproduced in this book. It was made in the late 40s/early 50s.

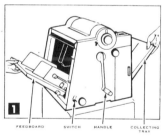

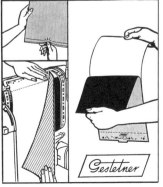

SPECIAL THANKS FOR HELP AND ENCOURAGEMENT

Everyone at Nettwerk Productions
for putting up with the ink smell,
Bart Campbell, Pina Campbell, Rudolf Penner,
Terry McBride, Cathy Barrett, Tom Harrison,
John Rummen, Mary Lynk, Peter Gzowski,
Tom Bagley, Molly Kiely, Judith Beeman, Tom Snyders,
Trent & Denise at Black Sheep Books Vancouver,
Michael Rummen, Tracy Marks, Ron Stelting,
Adam Drake, Kenn Sakurai, Janet Forsyth, Blaine Kyllo,
Jeffrey Weinberg, Alison Rogers, the Alfonso family,
cool shops & cafes that display my zine,
the kind folks along the way who've donated ink & paper,
and especially everyone who's taken a chance
and subscribed to
RALPH (Coffee, Jazz and Poetry).

This book is a collection of the first 25 issues of RALPH, reproduced in their entirety. Some addresses may no longer be valid so please enquire ahead of time before ordering anything. The scrapbook material (press clippings, posters, poems, photos, and illustrations) is from 1992-95 in keeping with the time frame that this book covers. The Molly Kiely illustrations on pages 116, 117 and 124 were drawn especially for this book because one can never have enough of her fantastic artwork! All illustrations and photographs are copyright the individual artists and photographers.

DISCOGRAPHY

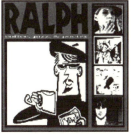

1. Looking For A Seat 2. This Dominion 3. Performance 4. SPOKEN INTRO 5. Sundays At The Stem 6. SPOKEN INTRO 7. Sunday At Newport 8. SPOKEN INTRO 9. Paris In September 10. SPOKEN INTRO 11. Chet Baker's Cigarette 12. Ring The Bells 13. I Love You Baby, But You Gotta Stop Wearing Those Ugly Shoes 14. OOH LA LA, C'est Comme Ca 15. A Long Kiss In The Rain 16. SPOKEN INTRO 17. Let's Fall In Love 18. Why Shouldn't I? 19. Somewhere At The End 20. SPOKEN INTRO 21. The Gargoyles Come Down From The Cathedral At Night 22. We're The People That Love Forgot 23. SPOKEN INTRO 24. Where Are The Bumper Boats In Salmon Arm, BC, Baby? 25. SPOKEN INTRO 26. The Goatee Club 27. It's A Wonderful World If You Know Someone In It 28. SPOKEN INTRO 29. Crawling Around In The Fountain 30. This Is My Corner Of The World 31. January's A Good Time For Jazz 32. SPOKEN INTRO 33. That's The Moment That I Fall In Love 34. The Day We Met, The Week We Spent 35. SPOKEN INTRO 36. Ti Amo Perche 37. SPOKEN INTRO 38. E Sempre L'Italia Nel Mio Cuore/There Is Always You In My Heart 39. Opportunities In Misery 40. Sunshine For Flowers 41. I Would Really Like To Kiss You, But I Can't See Without My Glasses

COFFEE, JAZZ, AND POETRY
June, 1995
Cat No: BB 1955 2

RALPH
with special guest...
STEPHEN QUINN
Guitar

1. introduction 2. My Way Of Giving 3. Olympia '66 4. There Is No One Here When I'm Dancing With You 5. Twist At St. Tropez 6. Bright Colours 7. Til The End Of The Day 8. Brighton Mist 9. Vox Guitars 10. Gloria Drank Dirty Water On Her Way to The 99th Floor 11. Bongo Beat

OLYMPIA '66
April, 1996
Cat No: BB 1956 2

1. Parlez Vous Jazz? 2. Halifax 3:AM 3. The Thirsty Club 4. Venus In Violets 5. Roman Intro 6. Roman Guitar 7. Sophisticated Boom Boom 8. Private Detective 9. If I Could Forget You (You Know I'd Be Glad To) 10. The Girlfriend's Club 11. Ocean At Night 12. Say Whatever You Want 13. Charlottetown Is Burning Down 14. Gene Vincent Died In My Arms Last Night 15. Happy With Nothing 16. Record Collectors 17. I'll Remember 18. Jangly Love Song 19. Maybe Ontario 20. Angels Going Home 21. Prince Of The Miramichi 22. C'est Jolie Noel/Christmas Is Nice 23. My World Of Suede 24. Tired Of Waking Up Tired 25. St. John's Beautiful Daughters 26. Early Morning Cold Taxi 27. I've Gone Blind and I Gotta Drive All Night 28. This Song (Is Just Like Every Song On The Radio) 29. Invisible Life 30. Saturday's Angel

INCLUDES BONUS MULTI-MEDIA MATERIAL
with 6 extra audio tracks (When Astrud Gilberto Sings, We Were So Pretty When, That's The Drag About Love, I Clean The Books That Nobody Wants, I've Gone Blind And I Gotta Drive All Night, I Want More Of What They Call Amore)

SOPHISTICATED BOOM BOOM
August, 1997
Cat No: BB 1957 2

ORDERING INFORMATION:
CDs can be purchased by calling 1-800-494-2770 (Outside Music).
You can also purchase these CDS directly from the author.
For further information, including subscribing to RALPH, please write:
Ralph Alfonso, Box 505, 1288 Broughton, Vancouver, BC, Canada, V6G 2B5
Email: ralpha6982@aol.com • Web: Http//www.bongobeat.com

If you enjoyed this book, please write or call
for a complete mail order catalog of beat related
books, magazines, videos, and much more.
We specialize in beat and alternative literature.

WATER ROW BOOKS
PO BOX 438, Sudbury, Ma, USA, 01776

TEL: 508-485-8515
FAX: 508-229-0885
Email: waterrow@aol.com
Web: Http://www.waterrowbooks.com